Goodbye, Amelia.

fictions
Simone Felice

The author wishes to thank Shel Silverstein for *A Light in the Attic*
(Harper & Row, 1981)

Selections from this collection have appeared in the following publications:
An excerpt from "Eight Subsequent Rooms" in *Hunger Magazine*, No. 8, 2001
An excerpt from "The Walker" in *Hunger Magazine*, No. 10, 2002
"A Brief Debriefing" in *Chronogram*, October 2002
"Out the Train Window" in *Prima Materia*, Volume 2, 2003
"Yesterday," "Out on the Beachscape," "I'd Love to Pull You Out of the Scenery,"
and "She's Been Running" in *Metroland*, May 2003
"On the Sickman's Machine" and "Amnesty from the Fingers" in
Fire, Spring 2004 (United Kingdom)

GOODBYE, AMELIA.
FICTIONS

Published by
Bliss Plot Press, PO Box 68, Mt. Tremper, NY 12457
Editor/Publisher: Brent Robison
Associate Publisher: Wendy Klein

ISBN: 0-9718908-2-X
Library of Congress Control Number: 2003108230

Printed in the United States of America

Cover art "The Fecundity of Chaos" © 2000 by Jordin Isip, www.jordinisip.com
Cover design by Melinda Beck, www.melindabeck.com

Author photo © 2003 by Theresa Ortolani, www.theresaortolani.com

First Printing

This book is for my folks.

Blue blue windows behind the stars / Yellow moon on the rise / Big birds flying across the sky, throwing shadows on our eyes / Leave us helpless

—Neil Young

The killer is never hunted. I never heard what sort of oil he has. Exception might be taken to the name bestowed upon this whale, on the grounds of its indistinctness. For we are all killers, on land and on sea.

—Herman Melville
Moby Dick

Hours of time on the telephone line / Talk about things to come / Sweet dreams and flying machines in pieces on the ground

—James Taylor

Goodbye, Amelia.

fictions

Book One

Goodbye, Amelia.
A Novella

Book One
Goodbye, Amelia.
A Novella

Goodbye, Amelia.

1

He was wearing his overalls when they came to take him away. The knock on the door so different from any other. Conspirator, they charged. Murderer. Anti-patriot. He got on his hat and rubber boots against the February outside and poured a little more coffee against the February inside and he didn't say a thing. He left the girl aching in the doorway of the farmhouse and he went on down the gravel walk with the ugly ugly men and he eased into their car and he never came back.

He left the flat in the afternoon of the day before and walked over to the bakery and sat waiting at one of the little tables for his friend Elton who was late but who he knew would come. The girl who put bread into bags always watched him when he was there. She wore her hair up and she moved quick and she had eyes like a mean bird but he knew the girl was harmless. The place was busy and it smelled good and warm and he sat there with his hands together listening to the sounds that people make and after a while the girl came over to him.

—Are you praying? she asked and she set down a small plate with a scone and a glass of water.

—I didn't ask for anything.

—You looked empty. Eat something.

—I'm waiting for someone.

—So eat to pass the time.

—What do you do?

—I work here. I give people bread and they give me money but the money isn't mine.

—And what do you do to be free?

Elton came in the side door. His face was red from the cold but it didn't look bad and he walked on to where Payne sat talking with the girl. He saw him and stood up and the two embraced.

—Sit down, said Payne. They sat.

—Who's this? asked Elton.

—She works here.

Elton didn't say anything.

—I have a telescope and my bathroom window goes out to the roof, she told Payne and she left them there and returned to her place behind the counter.

—Did you do it? asked Payne. His voice was low.

—It's done.

—Good. How many did you kill?

—Four.

—Good.

—They begged.

—They always do.

Payne leaned in and took his friend's head in both hands and looked into his eyes and there were the fiery clouds that owned Payne as well and he could hear nothing around him because he loved what they lived for like you'd love the worst part of a storm. He could smell the winter air that lingered on Elton's sweater, clean and volatile, and as he breathed it in he knew that he needed to be out of doors.

—Let's go, he said and took his hands from Elton's face.

Elton drank the water down fast and put the scone in his pocket and they rose to leave the bakery. Out on the sidewalk the two of them made their way downtown with the failing daylight lying in rays between buildings and shimmering in the water that lined the streets. Cars would pass and they would note the model and the look of the driver. They passed the movie theater and they passed the station and it wasn't long before they took up the little pathway that led along the river. They strode beside the handrail with the sun dying on their faces and the surface of the river looked fake from the influence of the same gaudy light.

—I'd like to see my mom, said Payne.

Elton nodded and they kept on. A man lay bundled and sleeping on the frozen ground that bordered the path and as they passed him he woke and looked up at them to see what they were and when it was clear he lowered his head again. The outermost layer of his bedroll showed a soiled pattern of badly imagined geese and Payne thought how nice it would be to fly away. Further up the river they began to see the haze of lights that came from the factory where Payne's mother worked at making plastics and paint since before he was alive. Soon they could see the sign on the main building that said UNITED and when they got to the entry door Payne told his friend to wait for him outside. He wouldn't be long.

He walked along the loveless corridor without looking at the notices that hung posted to the walls at random. One gave the details of an employee valentine party, another called for mandatory immunizations and listed the reasons why. People in baby blue uniforms passed him like lost animals in the hall and the numb smiles when they came only made him sad. Sad to think that these people had hopes. Sad to know that his mom's lungs hurt at night and that she loved France from the TV but would never see it. He got into the utility elevator and pressed the number 4 and the doors slid shut and he felt himself going up. He knew the pull in his stomach that lay coupled in his memory forever with the poor smell of the place and when the bell rang and the doors opened he came into the hallway thinking of how life gets trapped sometimes in boxes and closed spaces and he could hear his ten-year-old body running naked and crazy somewhere in the stale mazes of the United Paint and Plastics Company.

He came to a door that said PIECEMEAL and he opened it and went inside. It was a big room and he sought his mother out and went to her.

—What are you doing here? This is what she said every time he came whether she was happy to see him or not.

—When do you get out? Payne asked.

—Eight-thirty. And I'm going right home to soak my hands.

She looked old.

—I brought something for you, Mom.

He handed her a paper bag with a little less than ten thousand dollars in it.

—I already ate.

—It's not to eat.

—What is it, silly?

—Open it when you get home. Don't open it on the bus. Keep it in your purse.

—I should know if it's a bomb or a dinosaur egg or something. At least let me know what you've got me carrying all over God's earth against my will.

—Put it away, Mom.

A man came over to them. He was big and he wore the same blue as everyone else.

—Are you OK, Donna?

—Shame on you Glen, I would have thought you'd remember my son.

The man looked at Payne. At his rough beard. The overalls. His wild eyes.

—Oh, said Glen.

Payne wanted the man to go away.

—I'll see you at coffee, Donna. Don't be late.

—Thanks for looking after me, Glen.

—Someone has to, he said and went back to his station.

—Who the hell is that?

—Be nice, honey.

—I'm going, Mom. He kissed her on the cheek.

—I've got to get back to the line anyhow.

Thanks for the bag of secrets.

—Not till you get home, he said and turned to go but he stopped.

—Mom?

—What now?

—What would you buy if you could?

She breathed and turned the idea around in her mind.

—I would go get a good pair of shoes and I'd walk and walk. I'd walk until I couldn't hear anything but my heartbeat. No other sounds. Maybe a bird. And when I got there I'd rest. I'd rest awhile.

When he came outside he saw Elton leaning against the building with his hands in his pockets. He looked cold but he didn't say anything.

—How is she?

—She's tired, Elton.

Night had set in and they could see the lights of town calling and they started toward those lights, back along the river the way they'd come.

Town was quiet. They knew the man at the liquor store and as they came in he nodded and went on ringing up a group of young girls and he was ringing still when Payne and Elton walked out of the store with three bottles of wine and went on walking freely down the night street.

They found Elton's car in the back parking lot where he'd left it that day and they got in and Elton turned the engine and they drove the side streets until they hit the main road that led out of town and they drove on with the bottles resting on the seat between them. The car was a 1981 Oldsmobile and it was big and worn out and when they took up the back road that would bring them into the hills it ran loud and something smelled like burning but they knew it would be fine.

Payne took a corkscrew from the glove-box and opened one of the bottles. Their headlights shone far on the wet road before them and they could smell the wine now in the car, sweet in it's bad way, and Payne drank and handed the bottle to his friend and then he reached and rolled the passenger window down to let the night in and the wine burned familiar as it passed close along the border of his heart.

Mailboxes stood dumb along the roadside in that unsure place where the car lights met the darkness and then in the dark of someone's lawn Payne saw the thin form of a standing flag pole and he knew that there in the black above flew the colors of a nation. Colors that no one could see. A nation that he couldn't love. Not under the blackest disguises of night. Not in the high yellow grace of a million suns. He leaned and spat out the window and the Oldsmobile screamed it's thirsty scream as they slaved it across the land.

The land rose and then leveled off and there were no more houses and the bad road lay open before them. The radio played and now in the distance they could see the outline of the reservoir. It was half a mile wide and it was deep and still and this is where they came to be away.

As the car drew near it seemed as if the waiting body of water would close around them. Swallow them up. Wouldn't it all be so much lighter. They parked near the banks and Elton killed the radio but he ran the headlights a little longer and they sat drinking in quiet and watching the beams dance on the surface of the water.

An hour later Payne stood in the reeds that grew at the reservoir's edge. Does it stare into me? he was thinking. I stare into it. The February sky hung clear with its stars burning so far away and God burned further away. Elton leaned against the hood of the car smoking half of a cigar that he'd found. When he finished smoking he reached in and pulled another bottle off the seat and opened it and walked down to where Payne stood in the dark by the water. He let Payne have the first drink. The wine was colder now than it was before and it tasted good and went down easy. They stood talking for a long time about women. Then they talked about war.

—When do you think it'll end?
—Does it ever?
—This one, Payne.
—Which one?
—The one in the desert.
—Not until they take what they came for, I guess. Or until they choke on the piss of their own machine. But that could be a while.
—Do you think they'll come and take us?
—Not breathing. Hand the bottle over.
—White said they're taking everyone now.
—White is afraid. He's always been. He'll dance if they ask him.

A breeze came off the reservoir and they felt it touch them in the dark.

—If they still rode horses I would go, said Elton. Bad paintings and movies of such things rolled in his head. Payne shook his head and drank.

—I think it must have been different then, said Elton. —The world was different. Not so close. You could see what you were fighting. It had a name.

—It still tore you up, name or no name. It might have taken longer but you still saw your stomach and your own heart beating in the dirt ten feet away. You still screamed like an animal before you died.

—But there were things to hold on to. Ideas.

—Someone else's ideas. Someone who wakes in a bed and puts on good clothes and his body smells like fear and he talks in numbers and he is very far away from the screaming.

Elton took the bottle and drank the last of it and he was thinking about horses when they heard the car engine. They couldn't see it and then they could see it racing on the thin road that led along the water. It was them that it hunted.

They ran to the car and Payne threw open the door and pulled the guns from under the seat. The headlights found them. It was a big government car and they leaned behind the Oldsmobile and fired at it. At the windshield. At the tires. They heard the sound of bullets in the loose soil around them and then one hit their passenger window. They felt hot in their skin

21

and they kept firing. The government car lurched and turned a little and then it came to a sliding stop where the reeds began not far from the water. Its windshield was broken and it hissed and a man got out on the far side. He hid in the dark. They couldn't see him but they knew he was there. The driver was dead.

—Should we leave? whispered Elton. He was breathing hard and Payne saw the thing he feared. Saw it like a sickness on his friend's face. Like a sick yellow bulletin.

—He'll shoot the tires.

—What should we do?

—Kill him, said Payne. He put his finger to his lips to hush.

The man had crawled to the back of the car. He was shot in the left shoulder and his name was Michael Hudson and he had given his life over to those who would siphon the grace from it and he had two girls at home but they didn't know him.

They started shooting again, not sure of where he lay. The man returned fire and one bullet hit their back window and the other hit Elton in the throat. Payne could see the man now where he lay firing and he quickened and pulled Elton around behind the hood. He leaned against the metal of the car and aimed his gun at the man. He shot twice and both shots tore into Michael Hudson's face. He lay dead at the edge of the reeds and Payne pulled his friend into the car and drove away.

Elton was holding his neck with both hand and little wet noises came strange from him. He was bleeding bad. Payne held the wheel cursing and thinking of where they could go.

—Don't die, Elton. Don't leave.

Elton was still holding onto himself but he was quiet now and his eyes looked out into the shadows by the roadside. Payne knew a girl who lived on a farm maybe twelve miles away and he hammered on the gas and made the next hard left to head for it. The girl's name was Amelia Fisher and there was a time in his life when he thought he would die without her love but when she broke and placed it freely in his hand it withered there and after time she came to see the aching distance in him that kept his soul bound up in the wild skelter of the wind and she cried for him and for her own tied soul and for all the slaves in the world. And through the tears she told him that he couldn't love and she was right. Not that way.

Elton was dead when they got to the farmhouse.

—They won't get you now, babe, Payne said, choked in the dark. —They won't ever get you.

Amelia woke on the second floor to the lights and the mean rolling of the motor. She knew who it was and she came down the stairs and stood in the doorway. Payne closed the car door and came walking on toward the house.

—My father's asleep. He's been in bed with the flu.

—Elton's dead, Amelia.

She didn't say anything.

—He's in the car.

She stared past him.

—Get the car into the barn, she said. —

23

Pull the bay doors closed and latch them and get yourself inside.

He drove Elton's car around and brought it in through the big doors and he didn't look at the dead person on the seat. He killed the engine and stepped out into the cold dark. The barn smelled like rust and damp hay and he stood there sweating and as the sweat ran so did the years. He had chased her across the yard in the copper haze of a late summer gone and she hid in the barn and he found her there. They struggled. Her skirt had drawn up above her waistline and she hushed him and laid open the fair thing that beat between her legs like the pounding tides of a war that would not end and she worked the center of it with her fingers and she tore at the hair on the back of his head and pulled him to her and told him he could have anything at all. Anything at all.

The smell of coffee moved him as he came through the quiet house and he stopped in the entrance to the kitchen and stood there watching her make it. She let it steep a long time and then she took down two cups from where they hung on hooks and she poured the coffee into them and the steam came rolling. They sat at a small metal table by the window and they both looked a little insane and a little beautiful in their own private ways and soon the smallest hint of morning shone from the fringe of the world where her father's fields met the sky.

—Are you hungry, Payne?

—What?

—Are you hungry?

—All my life.

She didn't ask him how it happened and he wouldn't have known what to say if she had so they sat waiting for the coffee to cool.

Raw sunlight was passing faintly now through the frost on the kitchen window and Payne finished the bottom of his cup and put his head into his hands. He felt her touch his forearm. She gathered her strength and moved her hand up to rest it in his and he broke and held it there tight against the side of his head with the blood pounding. The refrigerator hummed and they were so young and the light was on their faces and hands and they were still holding on when they heard the car outside. And the boots on the walk. And the unbearable knocking at the door.

2

They killed people because they thought it might help to bring a little change into a sour world that had all but lost its meaning. They killed people for money to live. They blew up a toll booth. The robbed a small bank in another part of the state. They killed a millionaire at his country home on a lake and no one ever found his body. They blew an armored car to pieces in the middle of the night. They killed a news lady and they killed a deputy sheriff. They put a judge in the hospital for four months and his wife had died in the act. Sometimes they slept well at night, sometimes they couldn't sleep at all. They killed a lawyer and they killed the head of an investment firm and they killed a partner of theirs who would have turned on them. They killed a little bit of themselves everyday and they killed the pain with laughter and with alcohol and never once did they stop pretending.

Men from the Bureau came back to question Amelia and she told them half of what little she knew. She told them that she hadn't seen Payne in almost two years and that was true. He looked so desperate and tired when he came to the door that morning, she said. She felt so bad for him and that was why she let him in. She was terrified when they told her what was in the front seat of the car they'd found in the barn. They were friends when they were young, she told them, and she always knew he was wild but she didn't think he could ever hurt anyone. He used to keep pigeons and she would go help feed them and she didn't mind cleaning their cages. He would talk sometimes to the pigeons and he talked so kind. He would let them fly and they would be gone for days but they always came back. The government men sat in her father's living room listening to all of this.

—One time we found a pigeon dead in the morning and he took it in his hand and he couldn't look at me. I climbed down to let him be alone on the roof and I don't think he came down till the next day. I just can't see how he could hurt someone.

They told her to count herself lucky that she wasn't dead and they got up and put their hats on and told her that if they had any more questions they'd be back. She smiled and told them how grateful she was for their service and that it was men like them that kept America safe and true and they nodded and left mud on the throwrug as they shuffled out and when they were gone their smell stayed, danger and aftershave, and Amelia ran upstairs and locked herself in the bathroom and stood screaming into the mirror.

She thought that her screams might call back the little girl who had gone into the mirror and not come home. But the little girl was home. It is bones that grow. And glands that widen and change. Blood that turns wild or stale. Hair thickens and nails go long and legs lengthen and other blood finds its way between them. The child goes nowhere.

Amelia held on to the edges of the water-stained porcelain sink and she cried out for answers. When did her country first lay down with the greed thirsty cancer tired wolves who would teach it all the secret ways to go on eating its poor self alive so that they wouldn't have to die alone? When did the freedom leave? Where was the one she had loved so dear? Where were the days and where the hours of her life?

She walked over to the bathtub with her eyes crazy and red at the edges and she turned the hot and the cold and ran the water over her hand to check the balance in temperature. Too cool. She adjusted the cold again and returned her hand to its place under the faucet and she felt, after a moment, that it had gone a little too hot now but it would be fine after the drafts in the old walls made their own changes.

She sat on the edge of the clawfoot tub that had been in the house since it was built a hundred and forty years ago and she lowered her head into her hands. She brought her fingers through her hair and held them there tight against the hidden skin. The water in the tub was steaming. She freed a hand and lowered it into the tub and it almost scalded but she kept it there and she could feel the slight rising of the water.

She took her hand from the tub and got up. She walked over to the tall cabinet that stood near the mirror and she turned the latch and opened it. There were the powders and creams and razors and everything else. There was the simple hairbrush that her mother had left behind. In all these years she had never once touched it. She brought it out and closed the cabinet and stood in front of the mirror and she began to brush her hair. It was the color of raw charcoal and it was wild and she had never really loved it, although her father kept on swearing how pretty it was. If she ever did anything to make it nice she did it for him. She brushed now, but not for anyone. Just to know the bittersweet pull against the scalp and the slow rolling hand motions of comfort and instinct.

—Help me to bear this. Her dry voice came breathless into the air between her and the mirror. —You left me here. Now help me bear this.

She looked at the tub and saw that it had nearly run over and she set the hairbrush down and went and turned the water off. She reached into the bathtub and pulled up the plug to let enough water out so that she could get in and then she stood and took her clothes off. She pulled herself free of the thick wool sweater that smelled like everything she'd done or seen in the past two days. She kicked off her socks and her jeans and longjohns in two easy moves. She stood naked except for a worn out tank top. There were faint stains in the fabric from other years and it showed a tear in the left breast but it rested lovely on her shoulders and belly. She took it off. The steam rose up off the bathwater and she lifted a leg and placed it inside. It was too hot but she didn't care and she lifted the other leg now and stood there with her feet stinging and then she brought her whole body down into the bath. It hurt but the hurt was fine. She stretched her legs out and brought her spine to rest against the ceramic back of the tub and she felt her skin give as it became familiar with the burning circumstance.

She lay in the bathtub a long time and in that time she thought about many things but mostly she thought about her mother. Her name was Rose Marie. That was her mother's name.

—Come in, Amelia love.
—It's so cold, Mommy.
She stood at the muddy brink of the duck pond on the other side of their land and her mother called for her to wade out and join her where she stood waist high in the cloudy water. It was early spring and the sky lay pregnant with a dozen storm clouds rolling overhead and the water in the pond was icy cold but she didn't want her daughter to fear earthly things. Amelia was four years on the earth.
—It's nice when you get in.
The child shivered and stepped into the pond.
—Good girl. Now just walk like it was warm grass in the summer. Feel the grass.
Amelia felt the strange bottom give between her toes and she was scared but she walked on. When she reached the place where her mother stood she took hold of her naked leg and wrapped her tiny arms around it under the water. She held it. Her whole body ached. The water was up to her chin.
—I'm cold. Cold.
The woman pulled her daughter out of the pond and held her in her arms and walked with

her toward the shore.

—There are things inside of us, Amelia, she told her as she came to the shore. —Warmth and things that we don't know how to say. He have to find those things. We have to find them through the cold and through the fear that would claim us. We have got to find the warmth and hold on to it. If we can't then there is nothing for us here. If we can't then we run away.

And that's what you did, thought Amelia. Before that year was out. November, wasn't it? And Dad still dies every day when he wakes up and looks around your bedroom. Not because you're gone. It's not that at all. He dies because he can't remember your face. He dies every day because you never told us goodbye. The bath water had cooled a little but the lasting warmth of it surrounded her and she felt all right. Outside the sun had set and it was very dark now in the bathroom. Amelia sat up and reached for the lamp that rested on the short table against the tiled wall. She turned it on. She lay in the water and waited for it to go colder than her body and when it finally had she pulled the plug and rose from the bathtub. She took a towel from its place on the wall and dried herself with it. Then she turned the lock on the bathroom door and pulled it open and went on down the hall to find her bed. She had the towel wrapped tightly around her.

3

Wintertime tries to keep you inside. Their farmstand was closed until the end of April and there was not much to do until then. She read books and watched movies on the VCR. She read magazines. They couldn't afford a computer, or if they could her father with the hands like easy sandpaper said they couldn't. She kept the house nice and cooked almost every night and she took naps in the afternoon. She did little things to keep her mind off bigger things. And when none of this held weight anymore, she began to walk.

The beginnings of March can be as cold and mean as days in January. Sometimes it's worse because in January the winter hasn't had a chance to hold you under as long as it would like. March has a grip.

Amelia put supper in the oven to keep it warm for her father and she wrote him a note on the back of an oil bill. I'm out walking. I love you. Supper's in the warmer. Don't worry, I bundled up.

She went into the hall closet and found the basket with all the gloves and mittens and scarves and hats that had ever belonged to or ever been left in the house. She hunted through it and brought out what she needed. She ran upstairs and pulled on two sweaters. She found a pair of wool pants and pulled them over the pants she had on and then she came back downstairs.

She drank the rest of her tea that had been cooling in the kitchen and when the scarf and hat were in their right places she went to the door and pulled her boots on. She laced them and remembered the mittens. She walked back into the kitchen and took them from where they waited on the table and she got the mittens on and went outside.

It wasn't until she was down the walk and past the barn that she was met by the wind. There was a force in it and that force served to influence her movements. She thought she might blow away and then she knew she wouldn't. When you sleep inside of boxes you forget sometimes about the whirling. By the time she came to the end of the driveway she had learned not to fight against it but to let it guide her on and when the wind eased up she felt lonely and she missed it and when it circled again she was glad.

She walked out onto the country road that she loved because she knew it so well and because it had no yellow lines and because of the armies of forsythia bushes that ran along it on either side. The forsythia lay sleeping like a lot of things lay sleeping but she knew it would be waking early with the spring. She hadn't thought of where to go once she'd gotten to the road and it didn't really matter. She walked.

Cars were a rare thing on that road this time of year and she knew it so she walked in the middle and the only thing that felt cold was her forehead but she got used to it and then she didn't think about it. She could see the quiet road, long and straight before her. And then she saw where it began its rising far ahead.

She came to the crest of a hill and she stopped and looked out onto the wide farmlands. What remained of the old stone walls still ran long against the ground and sometimes they crossed each other where they met and now it all lay open to the eye like a cold gray quilt and the men who built those walls were gone and their first names were lost in the spaces between the stones. They'd built them because they needed somewhere to put the stone that they hauled from the earth as they cleared the land. They built them to show the lines of property.

She saw a brook that sprang from the high rocks off to the left of where she stood and the edges of it were still frozen but the center ran. She could see their neighbor's house and the wood smoke that came from the chimney and for all the chill that whistled round her, the sun shone clear and provocative in the bitter season. She walked into the landscape and the going turned easy as she started downhill.

On the flats a car came toward her and it stopped where it would have passed her. It was Kay. Kay was old and she live in the cottage behind the Briar House. She rolled down the window.

—Get in, child. You'll catch pneumonia.

—I'm just out walking, Kay. Thank you though.

—Out walking. Kay had to digest that one.

—Yes. Just out walking. I got tired of being cooped up inside. You know how that is.

—Not in the middle of winter.

—It's March.

—March don't care one bit.

—I needed air.

—Is there no air in your father's house?

—You know what I mean.

—Air is what gives you the pneumonia. You'll die out here in this.

—I'll be fine, Kay. Thank you for stopping.

Kay made a face and rolled the window up and drove off. Amelia kept on.

More than an hour later she came to an abandoned firehouse that stood falling into the roadside. Sometime in the seventies the volunteers had moved the company to a bigger, modern station near the post office seven miles away and they hadn't thought to tear this one down. Kids had broken all the windows and someone had fallen asleep drunk and crashed into the side wall and the place looked sad.

She stopped on the road and walked over and stood looking in through one of the vacant window frames. She saw the old fire helmets and fire jackets lying mildewed and frozen on the floor. They had left a small pump-truck that had become useless to them and now it stood in the cold and Amelia thought about how brief it is that we hold on to some things and how long it is that we hold on to others. But in the end, she thought, all of it gets left behind.

Someone had written FAGGOT in spray paint on the side of the truck and someone had written GO NAVY on the ceiling and Amelia looked at these things and then she turned and walked away from the firehouse and continued on the road.

Little birds sat shivering on telephone wires and she watched them as she walked. Why do they stay? Is it their memories that keep them?

They let the August rain come down warm against their skin. Come so lightly down with the late sunlight streaming careless through the trees, finding their wild faces to paint its amber shapes upon and all around them hung the brave smells of young sex and honeysuckle and earth and to be there one might have been coaxed into believing that maybe every last bit of hurt had finally gone out of the world. Maybe.
—Payne?
He look at the girl.
—Do you still believe in me? she asked.
—You're the only thing I've ever believed in, Amelia. He moved and kissed her.
—I want us to lay here forever, she said. —I want us to never die.
He laid his hand on her chest and waited to feel her heart beating there under his palm.
—Do you feel that? he asked.
—Yes.
—That kind of beating is the kind that lasts, he said. —We would be stupid to think it could die.
She found her own hand and brought it up against his heart.
—This is what we've been able to salvage, he said.
—What do you mean? But by now she didn't have to ask. These two could share a

thousand years of script between them and not say one word.

—*These crazy hearts. They're all we have left over from the trainwreck of this lying world. And no one can take them away from us, Amelia. No lawyer. No spies. No thieves in any uniform.*

—*I love to think of them always beating. Even after we're gone.*

—*They will.*

—*I know they will, she said.* —*They'll go on beating here in this field. And down at our spot by the river. On every street we've ever been. They'll pound in the back seats of Elton's old car someday when it's rusting in the junkyard.*

—*Don't let Elton know about that. He won't let us take it anymore.*

—*Lay still, she said and she stood up half naked and reached for her bag and pulled her camera out. It was older than she was and had seen more and she loved the hazy pictures it took.*

—*Please don't. Someone might use it against me. Hard evidence.*

His protest meant nothing and both of them knew it. He loved to watch her shoot. It's when she's really living, he thought.

—*Quiet, she scolded lightly.* —*You're not as bad as you'd like to think. You're just a naked boy to me.*

He laughed.

She began circling him. Taking pictures. Moving closer. Further away. She changed film. Shooting again. Dreaming that she might stop the time. Time that no one owned. Time that laughed like a crazy whore at those who would try and shackle it down.

She came too close and Payne took hold of her arm and pulled her to him and they rolled over together in the grass. Laughing. Sweating. Love their only burden.

—I want to go around the world, she said when they were still. —Will you come?

—How?

—It doesn't matter. We'll just go and get lost. I'll take pictures of everything everywhere. And I'll hold up all the prints to show the world how naked it really is. How beautiful. How wrong. That's all I'll ever need. To get lost in the world with you and this Pentax and nothing else would mean a thing.

Payne lay there quiet in the balmy light, half listening. He was tired of the future. Dreams at auction. Young man made weary by all the campaigns for a cleaner tomorrow. The bold promise. The filthy whisper. The slogans. Let me be, he told the whisper. Let me breathe.

—Payne. She touched him. —Where did you go?

—I'm right here.

—What's wrong?

—Me, he said. —Something in me.

The birds were gone now from the phone lines and the sun rested low in the sky and soon the colors began to show. The bleakest purple in the world became another purple and another purple and the winter sun fell into the far hills and the burning colors rolled into darkness. Amelia shivered. Any charity that had been offered in the daylight hours was gone now and half of the moon hung like a frozen road sign so that those who went on two feet would not mistake the severity of their choices and this one walked long into the night alone.

A doe and two fawns passed her as she came up the driveway. It was close to midnight. Her father was sitting in his chair and he was looking into the small open door of the wood stove when she came into the house. She untied her boots and got them off. Most nights he was in bed before ten. She went into the living room and sat on the rug by his feet. He looked at her.

—You're still alive. His face was lit by the fire in the stove.

—You better hope I am.

—How was your walk?

—Good. How was the chicken?

—I didn't eat much. Where did you go?

—I took our road out past the Briar farm and the firehouse. Then I turned left on the county road and made the whole loop and got onto the other back road and came over the two bridges and around the marsh and back home. Do you know you can still smell the sulfur in the winter?

He nodded.

—And I stopped to look at a few things on the way. Things that caught my eye.

—I worry.

—You shouldn't, Dad.

Something popped inside the fire and they looked into it.

—Dad?

—What.

—Why did Mom leave?

He looked at her.

—You know why she left, Amelia.

—You told me that she was miserable. That she wasn't happy on the farm. A lot of people live their whole lives unhappy.

—She just wasn't happy.

—That's not enough.

She was asking for something that he knew nothing of. He didn't know the woman. They met on the train. She had been visiting family upstate and he was bringing two cases of cider to the outdoor farmers' market in New York and the train was full so they ended up next to each other. She was tired of the city at that time so she married him and came to live on the farm and they made a baby and he got up everyday before the light and came in after sunset and he had no idea who the woman was. Rose Marie. That was it.

—It's enough for me, he lied.

—I don't think it is.

—How could you know?

—I know that you miss her. I've tried to be everything for you.

He reached for her hand and held it.

—And you have, sweetheart. You have been everything.

—I haven't been her.

He held the tears.

—She's dead to us. She's been dead to us twenty years. You're all the light I ever needed in the world. You. You mean all the world.

She gripped his hand and put her head against his knee. She stayed on the floor and cried but he would not. Not to save his life.

—What did she love? she asked through the tears.

—Please leave it alone.

—What did she love?!

—I guess if I knew then she might still be here.

—What called her?! What could have called her away from us?! What did she love more than us?!

The tiny riot in the fire was the only sound in the house now. Father and child had collapsed in on themselves and the vacuums that lasted robbed swiftly to render their bodies quaking and starved for sound.

—What do we name her? he asked.

Rose Marie lay drenched and exhausted and this was the last thing she cared to think about. She didn't answer. The doctor had gone out to let them be alone. She held the wrapped up thing against her chest and its tiny heart pounded and it cried a while and then it rested quiet. The young man looked helpless where he sat sweating in the hard chair against the bed under the warped revelations of the hospital fluorescents.

—What will we name her? he asked again.

—What do you like? Her voice came from so far away. He thought about it.

—My grandmother was Kathryn. I loved her as much as anything.

—That's not it. Kathryn is wooden.

He nodded.

Goodbye, Amelia.

—She needs a good name. One with gravity, said Rose Marie.

—Have you been thinking on it?

—No.

The lights were bearing down on them and they kept sweating but the room felt so cold. So white. So clean and scrubbed. So hollow.

—Should we call the nurses in to change the sheets? he asked. The young man felt the fool.

—Amelia.

—What? He couldn't hear all of it.

—Amelia. Amelia. Amelia and maybe she'll fly away.

They held each other in the living room. The fire burned humbly now and cast its meek shadows on them where they sat arm in arm, her head against his thigh. The woman who had passed through their home and through their lives like a windstorm was gone and she would stay gone. And like a windstorm, she held those qualities that beg for the uprooting and misplacement of things and in that whirling seizure it so happens that the very lightest of victims are cast into the soil at the fringes and here these things grow in a manner that is out of keeping with a course that would have seen them belted down onto the heartless runway of order and palsied fate.

4

John Sparrow talked with The Devil while he fished. It is to be assumed that The Devil did not talk back, being most days out of earshot, shaking hands and whispering, whispering into corners and kissing babies and standing at the head of tables the world wide, calling out loud for sway; the great orator on business that pressed more than one man's loneliness.

—Do you lose things? John Sparrow asked anyway. Small waves touched the rotting posts of the long dock. —Does your head hurt? I've had the same headache since nineteen seventy. Don't you remember me? I was the fool in the helicopter. A thousand and eighty days in that beautiful piss-poor country and I seen you more times than one.

His fishing line showed itself slack twenty yards out where it met with the water and it danced there and he watched it dance, sitting on the weathered boards at the edge of the dock with his legs hanging down and his hands holding onto the pole by the cork under the reel under the fog-colored sky.

—I seen you in the whorehouse. We passed in the upstairs hall and you called me by name. You had a drink in your hand and you looked sad and the whore on your arm was half dead with fever. Where did you go that night? I sure had a time.

—I thought I seen you carrying a burned child after a bomb exploded in the market a week later. You were burned too. Everyone was crying. Looking for their own. The smoke. Men lay without legs in the smoke. The smoke and the heat and the narcotic smell of all the flowers that grow there because they must, grow on through all the fire-haunted nights, alive in the perfect danger. Where did you take the child? Was it yours? Was it part of you?

—I would hear you cutting in and out over the radio in the chopper. Sometimes you would sing. Sometimes I miss it. The screaming wildness of the whole goddamned thing

He felt a tug at the line. He pulled and checked. He checked again but nothing was there.

—You came to me in the jungle, didn't you? You came as ten thousand dragonflies and I was drugged and you touched me and I dreamed I was very young in the library of the town where I was born. I opened a book and it hurt to read so I replaced it and took another and this new book was my own story. The whole story. What my father said to get my mother into bed and my paper route and how I would die and all the things in between. But I was in no library. I was with you in Cambodia where we shouldn't have been and my leg was broken and I was shot in the hip and the world was all morphine and you came and saved my life.

His hand quaked the slightest now and John Sparrow knew he had a fish. This time he had one. He stood up on the dock and took a breath in and the wild salt air told him he was still alive. He let some line out and watched for troubles in the water with his gray water-colored eyes.

The day was almost done and in the kitchen the failing sunlight came meekly through the old windows and rested in wide broken lines on the pine floorboards. John had the fish laid out dead on newspapers on the table. His sleeves were rolled up over his elbows and he was dressing the animal skillfully with a long wood-handled fillet knife that he cared for dearly, having opened more than their share of bellies together.

—You put up a fight, he told the fish. —A good goddamned fight.

But the fish, its guts on the man's table, just stared out blind past the small windows and down and beyond to where the ocean broke against the shore and to where an untouchable piece of its splayed self now moved in secret bodiless union with the waves and whatever it is that provokes the waves.

When he had finished he rinsed the knife under the faucet in the basin sink and went upstairs. He felt her on the handrail and then heavier in the narrow hall on the way to their— his bedroom. Underfoot, the boards of the floor creaked easily as he went and the well worn sound of it was not unpleasant but John Sparrow heard nothing. Every year that followed the war would come and leave with a little bit of his already maimed hearing, a constant passing into further echoes, until all that remained for the pilot was a great inarguable hush, the uneasy peace of the recent deaf, and the sometimes inward coup of whispers whispering old tender promises and the crying metal of helicopter blades and the screams of boys screaming don't let me die.

Some things can't leave.

He opened the door and came into the simple room where he slept or couldn't sleep and there she was and was not. On the old brass bed. Lying on it. Face down. Face up. Curled into a ball. Sitting at the edge. Facing the door. Facing the window. Lying on the floor. Up against the wall. Asleep. Dead. Laughing. Standing out on the rotting balcony that led from the room. Looking down onto the cliffs. Out to the water. In at him. Up into the twilight. Crying. Singing. Gone.

—It was a fine day by the water, he told the absence. —I hooked a pretty one. Small but pretty. Not too small. It was a queer color, not in a sick way. A nice color.

He walked over to the bed and sat on the light wool blanket that covered it and he unbuttoned his shirt and hung it on the bed post and then he pulled his shoes from off his feet.

—No sign of her yet, said John to the absence. —Not a whisper. Do you think she'll ever find this place?

He looked out past the open French doors to the small balcony, the cream paint peeling.

—It was a fine spring day. I wish I could say not a cloud in the sky but I would be a liar. It was gray as ever but not bad gray. It was fresh and got cold toward the end. It was a fine day for casting. Not much wind at all.

He walked over to the balcony doors and he closed and latched them and returned to the bed. He lay down on his back now, his weathered head on the thin pillows, elbows out and fingers laced beneath the base of his skull. He breathed easily.

—I had a long talk with The Old Crow, he said. The Old Crow is what he'd come to call The Devil. —I had some things to clear up. A few misplaced pictures rattling around inside my useless head. I need to do something with all those pictures.

Twelve minutes later he was fast asleep, his broad army chest rising and settling and rising again, half reluctant to the call of its own measured tempo.

5

She walked everyday until the weather broke.

Spring came late but it did come. The smells. The smells and the cool easy feeling and the rains. The rain and the sound it makes in the gutters and on the roofs and the new look of things and the fresh breezes. People in light sweaters. People outside. People smiling for no reason at all. The air and the ground, soft and pregnant, and the wet streets and the cool electric nights.

Her aunt Maureen had died when Amelia was twenty and that was when her father asked if she would take over the running of the farmstand and she did.

She hadn't seen Lilly since they closed the stand just after Halloween and they met there in the morning and began to do what had to be done before they could open for the season.

Lilly worked weekends until school ended and then she worked every day but Tuesday. She had been with them for three summers and she talked a lot and flirted with customers but she was strong and they trusted her and she worked hard. They liked Lilly.

Paul Fisher owned a little more than eighty acres of good workable land that ran along their road and spread back far into the woods and that old road lead through the flats and then the hills between the river and the high rocky incline where the ridges of the mountain rose in their abrupt way and on that land he raised the things his father had. He raised strawberries and those were the first to come. People would stop and pay a set price to spend a while in the fields picking their own or you could buy them at the stand for three dollars a quart. He raised eggplant and squash and melons and tomatoes and three different kinds of greens. Sweet corn and Indian corn and peas and onions and potatoes and alfalfa for hay and as feed for the cows. In the fall he raised pumpkins and gourds and he tapped the old grove of maples near the house for syrup and he boiled it himself and sold it in jars at the stand. They did well in the fall. Most of their business at the stand was from city tourists who stopped for country things as they came through on their way to other places.

In the good weather the cows lived outside and twice a day they brought them in for milking. Because of the federal regulations, the milk could only be sold to a large dairy conglomerate who would see that it was properly pasteurized and packaged and distributed according to the new guidelines. The trucks came every other day for pickup and this helped to bring money in but under no circumstances were they allowed to bottle the fresh milk and sell it at the stand in its raw form.

Paul had three Mexicans and a local kid named Billy to help him on the farm. They worked the small hand planter on the short rows and they drove the tractor that pulled the big planter along the main rows as it lifted up the soil and laid down the seed and fertilizer in a triple-15 blend and then covered it over again. They did all the weeding and the picking by hand and they cleaned and washed what they picked so that it could be sold at the stand and once a week two of them drove a small shipment to the city for the market that ran in the summer months. They did the milking and the feeding and they used the manure on the fields, pulling the spreader behind the tractor to lay it evenly as fertilizer. In the fall they helped him with the soil testing that was done to check for the right concentration of minerals. Nitrogen, potassium, phosphorus and others. And when the tests came back they read them to know how best to rotate the crops come spring. They helped the girls at the stand when it got busy on the weekends and they did everything else that needed doing. He paid them all well and treated them with respect and what he expected from them was a good day's work, everyday. No more and no less. He was a quiet man and they didn't try to understand his quiet ways but he worked as hard as they did and he was fifty-eight years old. The workers were fond of Paul Fisher.

He came driving down the thin dirt road that led from the big cow barn to the farm stand. He pulled the pickup in front. The girls were coming from the shed in the back carrying the large baskets that they used to put potatoes and onions in. They were laughing.

—What's so funny? he asked, stepping out of the truck.

—Nothing, Dad, said Amelia. —Lilly's just

as crazy as always.

—I was telling her about the exchange student that my Mom has staying at our house this quarter. He brushes his teeth with soap, Mr. Fisher. Regular soap. I saw him rubbing the bar on his toothbrush in the morning and I almost died and then when he put it in his mouth I started laughing at him and he got so embarrassed, I guess, so I told him that it was all right but he didn't like me after that and now he doesn't talk at dinner and my Mom's mad at me. He's from Croatia. That's in eastern Europe.

—Did you get the shed aired out?

—The windows are open and the back door but it always takes a couple days, Amelia told him. —We're getting out all the baskets and the big bins and then we'll dust them off. I'm always amazed at how much dust settles over the winter.

—Should I send Carlos to help you with the corn bins?

—We can handle it, Dad.

—I've been lifting weights.

—I'm pleased to hear that, Lilly. If you two need anything, I'm over with the cows. The vet is coming this afternoon.

—Is something wrong?

—No, no. Just their spring check-up. Rose is tired. I doubt she'll last the summer, but that's natural. She's old and been good to us. Other than her, they all seem real strong. I'll see you later.

—I might be out. Lilly wants to take me driving. She just got her license.

—I passed the first time. I forgot to use my

signals but I think the Man thought I was cute.

—She's going to drive me into town when we finish here. There's a new movie at the Orpheum that we might see.

—Be careful, both of you.

—I'm good, Mr. Fisher. I am. I don't forget the signals anymore and I do the speed limit.

—I'm sure you're fine, Lilly. It's the other fools on the road that worry me.

—She's in good hands, Dad. I'll be co-pilot.

She kissed him and he turned and walked over to the truck and climbed in and he waved with his big hand out the window as he drove off.

—Your Dad's cute.

—Yeah, said Amelia. —He is.

They brought out the rest of the baskets and wiped the dust from them with a wet rag and Amelia checked the old cash register to make sure it still opened and closed all right. Lilly sprayed and wiped the small pane windows on either wall and then she swept the floor and swept behind the counter while Amelia began writing out strawberry prices on a chalkboard. When they were done they closed up and walked around to the back of the stand where Lilly had parked alongside the shed. They got in and pulled their seatbelts on. Lilly looked at herself in the mirror and then she turned the key and the engine turned over and they heard the car running.

—Ready?

—Lilly. She looked at her where she sat. Her hands, lovely on the steering wheel. There was such a nice color in her face. —I'm so glad to see you growing up.

—Me too.

They drove for more than half an hour and when they got into town they found a place to park not far from the old theater. They locked the doors of the car and walked easily down the street. There was no rush. The movie started in ten minutes and there was still some daylight left and they stood outside the place talking and feeling good.

Lilly looked in at the clock through the heavy glass doors and saw that it was time and she asked Amelia if she was ready to go inside.

They got their tickets and Lilly bought a box of red licorice and they went down the carpeted hall and into the dark theater and they found two seats in the back and sat down.

It was a movie about a man who had been a famous piano player in Warsaw, but his family and his musical life had been stolen from him during the occupation of Poland. He spent a long time hiding. In empty apartments. Forsaken places in the walled ghetto. Finally inside the city proper. He stayed fed by the goodness of others and he stayed alive by his own grace and by his dead belief that there would come a day for him to be let free.

In one part, the Germans had him running through abandoned buildings and in his running he came upon a piano in the dark. The thing that he had lived for solely, before the war took all. The very thing that he was made to abandon. And there in the dark he held the urge to lay his hands on it for fear of being found out. But this man stayed and hovered above the instrument's body and there he feigned his playing with his fingers tearing at the air and he alone in all the world heard the ringing of the keys. No Nazi heard.

It was a very good movie, beautiful and it broke your heart, and they left the theater thinking and feeling fine and the feeling followed them well into the night.

6

She finished adding up their total on a piece of paper; the register only half functioned. It opened easily and closed into place with a loud click but the numbers hadn't worked in years. She took their money and was putting everything they bought into a brown grocery bag when she saw Sweet Walter pull up in front. He almost hit the customers' Volvo. Amelia smiled.

—Oh, I didn't see the preserves. Did you, Honey?

—No. The woman looked around. — Oh, there they are, hiding behind the counter.

They were a smart looking couple in their thirties. Amelia had seen them there the year before.

Walter came walking over but he stopped and stood touching things, pretending to browse. He didn't want to disturb the transaction.

—Yes. I'm sorry. We're just getting things sorted out here. She went to the jars and picked them up to read the labels. —We have peach. Black currant. Pear. And strawberry of course. A friend of ours does all the canning. She comes with different stuff. Sometimes she brings pickles and pickled beets and tomato sauce.

—Well, we'll have two strawberry and one peach, said the woman.

—Add another jar of the peach, please, the

man told Amelia. Then he turned to his wife. —I have to bring something home for your Mom, or we'll never hear the end of it. And she goes crazy for good preserves.

—You're always thinking of Mom. Why did you marry me? she joked.

—You were the easy one.

She slapped his hand lovingly.

Amelia took the four jars and put them into their own bag.

—That's just another twelve dollars, please. Don't worry about the tax.

The man handed her a ten and a five and told her to keep the change and they thanked her and told her they would be passing through again sometime in the fall and that they would surely be stopping for the famous pumpkins. Amelia told them that the same lady who did the canning also baked pumpkin pies and brought them in for sale on the weekends in September and October and the couple was doubly excited. They thanked her again and walked happily to their car. They put the things they'd bought into the back of the Volvo and they got in and went on their way.

—I've been wondering when you'd be coming in to haunt me. It was the first time she'd seen him this spring. —Is it really you, Sweet Walter? Are you really real?

She touched his arm and smiled.

—I've never been all too sure of that fact, Amelia.

Sweet Walter stood with his hands in the pockets of the gray uniform slacks that he wore for his job. These were the only clothes she had ever seen him in. He was past sixty and for as long as Amelia could remember he had worked in the tollbooth at the big suspension bridge that spanned the river twenty miles away. The bridge led out and joined with the interstate highway on the other side of the river. Walter worked on this side. He lived alone with his mother who he claimed he took care of. She was very old but she was very healthy and Amelia knew that it was probably the other way around. Sweet Walter was a rare thing.

—Is the bridge still standing?

—Why must you fool with me?

—I'm just asking. I can't remember the last time I crossed it.

—The bridge is fine, Amelia. The bridge is always there. I, on the other hand, have been fighting a very ugly cold.

—We're always fighting something, I suppose.

—And you, my dear? How is miss Amelia?

She breathed in and as she did she felt her heartbeat change and her hands go cold.

—I've had a hard time, Walter. In the winter, I mean. Toward the end. She paused. —I guess I feel better now. I think I do. Yes. I feel a lot better, she lied.

—It gets bad in the winter. I know. I turn the little heater as high as it goes. But the wind still finds me in the booth. And nobody looks at me. They hand the change over and they roll the window up so fast and they never look at me in the winter.

He thought.

—I spend my life touching people's hands.

And they touch mine. But only for that short time, Amelia. I don't get to know them. Where do they go? Everyone has clouds in their eyes. They drive up and the window comes down and we touch for no time and then they pass away. But where do they all go?

Amelia didn't know.

—I love you, Sweet Walter.

She hugged the man. He kept his hands in his gray pockets but it felt so good to have her against him. She smelled so new.

A van full of people pulled along the side of the road by the farm stand and one of them shouted out that they were lost and could they please have directions. Amelia shouted back and told them that she had never heard of the place they were looking for but that she could tell them how to find the closest primary road. They said that they had just come from there and that the place they sought could be found on no map.

Amelia and Sweet Walter looked at one another and then they looked at the van again. It was a light cream color, and very clean. The people in the back seats looked clean and they were all smiling but the smiles were the kind that turn the stomach. The kind that could be read like a leaflet. The kind that someone else owned and that someone had come to dictate down to the arc of the smallest muscle in the face.

—Won't you come along, children? shouted the driver of the van. He had a kind face.

—What do we say? Walter asked Amelia. His voice was hushed and he looked uncomfortable standing there.

The driver asked again.

—We're very busy, Amelia shouted.

—Too busy for Him? He is patient but His patience grows thin in the hour of our folly.

—We have a lot to do here today. Thank you, though. I hope you find what you're looking for.

—Oh we will, said the man. —We go to The Light Everlasting, child. A storm is coming near to this place. It's been long coming. I pray It be merciful with you.

The van drove away.

—How do people get that way?

Sweet Walter thought about this. His dusty white eyebrows worked and so did his forehead.

—I guess maybe they forget themselves. Or they're afraid of what they'll find if they look at their own dreams. They hide them away.

He paused for a long time. Amelia knew that there was more and she waited.

—Maybe they give their selves over but they don't know it. If you asked them when or where they left it they would look at you funny. It must be a whole lot easier to go riding in someone else's dream.

Amelia looked out across the fields and saw her father there, walking between the rows. Every hundred feet or so he would kneel down and touch something but she couldn't see what it was that he touched.

It was dirt. He turned it in his hand. Just to feel it there. Just to know it would stay.

7

This old house. This old weary off-white house in the state of Maine with its one naked pear tree suffering in the rocky yard and its big crooked front porch that faced out east into the always rolling, sad and always winter-colored Atlantic.

John Sparrow came home from Vietnam in nineteen seventy-one and when they discharged him from the veteran's hospital he walked alone into the mean plastic roar of America and that roar breathed its restless hymn into the young man's crippled ears until it pushed him, at last, out to the rocky fringes of a country that knew nothing of what he'd lived through. A country that had been taught to know nothing of the world outside.

Sitting at his mother's table, lemonade, head pounding, hip aching, heart knocking, he tried to tell her what it was like, what he had seen and how it had been in his time away.

—Hot as Florida?

—You've got to talk louder, Mom.

—Like Florida?

—Hotter, Mom. Different. We tried to sleep days when we could. We tried to give 'em hell at night.

—Watch your mouth, she said, more from habit than any real censure.

—We gave it to them, all right, he had

said, quietly, his changed eyes fixed upon the garishly patterned orange and light purple curtains covering the window above the sink in his mother's kitchen, keeping away the kind rays of the afternoon sun. —Our boys rained The Orange down on their forests until there was no where left for them to hide. But they found new places, and they were mean little bastards. Stubborn. I guess you can't blame them. Fierce little bastards. And who was who? They came to blend into the towns. Into the city. The women too.

His mother watched her only son. His strange eyes on the curtain. What did they do to my boy? she thought. When did he stop running through the yard after fireflies?

—And they were hotter than the days. The women, I mean. I knew a guy. An officer. Nice guy. He fell in love with one of 'em. Head over heels. She said she wanted to come with him back to the States. She told him she was pregnant. He was gonna marry her. That's how much she got to him. She was awful pretty. Pretty color in her cheeks. The MP's found him one morning on a hotel floor with his throat cut open from ear to ear. She killed him like that for the maps he kept with him. Pretty bitch, huh?

His mother was crying now. Crying then. And here was her son more than thirty years later living the rest of his deaf life alone on the eastern coastline with little more than the sad government checks and his fearful love of the ocean to get him on through the days.

8

At four-thirty in the morning she woke in her bed. She had been dreaming and the aspect of it still hovered by her, but when she tried to pick out the details, the whole thing blew away like a breath of cigarette smoke turned loose in the driving rain and all that remained of the dream were the violent colors that had made up the border. Amelia could find no other sleep to fall into, so she left the bed.

She got dressed and went downstairs and, moving through the relative darkness, found her way to the windowed door that led out on to the back porch. She turned the knob and pushed the thing open and once outside she turned and closed it again, gracefully, and with no racket.

She walked over to the left of the big porch where a swing hung chained to a hook that had been screwed into a beam behind the wainscoting. It was worn out and most of the paint on the seat had flaked away and the swing itself creaked softly in its wide sway and she had loved it all the years of her life.

It moved a little in the little breeze that passed and Amelia took hold of the chain and held it still and sat down and she began to rock. It was lighter outside than it was in, that membranous light that shows a while before morning, and she could see the ghost of things around her. She smelled the lilacs dying sweet and sad on the bushes that surrounded the wooden rails of the porch. These had always been her favorite flowers but Lord they come and go so quick and maybe that's why. No time to tire. She used to bring them by the bushel into her room to try keeping them alive with light and water. She would leave the lamp on all night.

Out in the yard she could see her father's old pickup truck where it lay resting near the big willow tree, the easy branches spread like a canopy, ministering over it. She tried but she couldn't remember why he had parked it there and taken it off the road. It must have been ten years ago, she thought. More. I guess he needed something newer for the farm. We sure had good times in that ancient thing. I still know the way it smelled inside. Like Dad. Like paper coffee cups and dried mud on the floorboards. Like wind. It was so big inside and he always kept that turkey feather that he called an eagle feather hanging by a rubber band on the rear view mirror. We loved everything about that truck.

She looked over to the other side of the porch and there was the tired copper-colored birdcage that had hung for so long a time with no tenant and now both of them swung there in the half dark, empty girl and empty cage, each pendulum dumb to the needs of the other.

What was it about his face? she thought. Payne's face in the morning. That cold morning when the world took sick and strained to cry from under it's feversheets that it might need to stay February awhile.

Amelia couldn't shake it. It wouldn't go.

All these months and it wouldn't leave and there was nothing she could do but smuggle it away and wait like a midwife for it to scream again and lift it's head.

Something terrible there in that face. Something wicked. Some dark comrade of love that no prison could hold.

Something free.

How could you leave me here, Payne? What about our world? All the sunsets and the Beatles records and the suitcase full of negatives. Our lifetime of stills that we'll never hold.

And here I am with one picture left, my love. It's of you, sitting like a crazy orphan at my father's kitchen table, drinking my coffee and waiting for the world to either chant your name loud in the streets or forget the sound of it altogether and for keeps. Was the blood that good between your hands? What about our blood, Payne? What about my hands? Was it that holy? The killing. Holy enough that you had to come to me with it burned into your face? After all that time. Did you have to come back and pull me apart for good so that I might remember how it felt again to have my life on fire?

She tried looking up to where heaven ought to be and still the morning sun had given no sign that it existed anywhere out in the flat cobalt sky and as she rocked now on the swing, Amelia thought about how it might be if it didn't come.

But it comes.

In war and in peace. It rises up to see men

tortured within an inch of their lives and new brides kick their shoes off in the grass. The sun lights the stage. And it will until the last act, and after.

Halfway through breakfast Amelia asked her father about the truck.

—That thing's got to be deader than a doornail by now. It was nineteen eight nine I parked it there. I know 'cause that's the year of the new Dodge. Well not so new now. Besides, aren't you happy riding around with me?

—Of course I am.

—And I always give you the keys if you want to go someplace.

—That's not it, Dad. I just forgot how much we loved that old truck. And I was sitting on the back porch this morning, before you were up, and I saw it there and I thought how nice it would be to see it running again. I miss it.

—What's to miss? The heater only worked half the time in the winter. The same with the wipers. And the seats and the dashboard are all cracked and like I said, who knows how much it would cost to get it running again.

—I'll pay for the parts.

—And who's going to do the work on it?

—I was hoping you could show me what needed doing and I could do it myself.

—Jesus, Amelia. I'm no mechanic.

—You know enough. I see you working on the Dodge sometimes and on the tractors with Carlos.

—That old truck needs more time than I got.

—I told you, just show me what to do.

—You don't give up.

—At least have a look at it one of these nights. Please.

—You never give up.

—Thanks, Dad. She reached over the table to kiss him.

—I didn't say I would. And don't kiss me.

She kissed him anyway.

9

Thursday afternoon it rained and she closed the stand early. It was the cold kind of spring rain that no one wishes to be out in.

Amelia dragged the baskets inside and she could hear the tiny explosions of raindrops tap tap tapping away on the tin roof. Billy and the Mexican they called Tio came to help her with the rest and it had turned into a downpour by the time they'd finished.

They stood out of the rain.

—Thanks, Billy. Thank you, Tio. You didn't have to make a special trip all the way over here. I would have been fine. It's only water.

—Mister Fisher sent us, said Billy. He seemed a little hurt.

—And I'm glad you came, Billy. I'm always happy to see your face.

Billy blushed.

—I just know how much else there is to do.

—It's no problem, said Tio. —No problem.

—He said we should drive you up to the house.

—I think I'll walk, Billy. But I thank you both very much. You've been a great help.

—Walk? Tio was shocked. —We cannot allow it. We will drive you.

—No, really. I've got a raincoat inside. It's good for me. —Your father will be unhappy.

—He'll live.

Tio and Billy looked at each other and Billy shrugged his shoulders. They said goodbye and Amelia thanked them one more time and they ran through the rain and got into the Dodge and drove back to help the others fix a leak in one of the silos.

She got her raincoat on and pulled the hood up and closed the useless padlock on the worn out doors of the stand and she crossed the road and walked the half mile up to the house.

Brown water ran hard on either side of the driveway as she came walking. It tore into the dirt and the gravel and the dirt and the gravel could do nothing but give. She felt the rain driving down against the crown of her head where the thin plastic hood of the raincoat lay as a barrier of chastity between her and the frantic sex of the sky. She tore it loose. And as she did, the downpour heaved and found the chance to beat its mindless timpani all through the black bramble of her hair. Her lawless hair.

She looked at her shoes and then she looked at the warring clouds and the bursts of light that shone electric between them. Behind them. She held out her hands and studied the veins that ran. O, the lines that run.

And in these moments, everything in her immediate universe screamed with life and it felt so good. Time and fate were dead in the downpour and she could have been anyone there. Any woman at any time. It could have been grain that she carried. Or furs or beads or bright feathers. It could have been an umbrella or it could have been a dead child that she carried, walking through the rain. A box, a cabbage, a shovel, a pen, a camera, an apple, a matchbook, a starfish, a brand new baby boy. Leg shackles, hand shackles, neck shackles, whiplash and rope burns, wide open red and stinging in the rain.

She could have carried a letter in her pocket. A song in her heart. A hand full of seed or a crust of bread. A basket of fish, a coin, a diary, a locket, a violin, a pear, a key chain, a pamphlet, a clock, a second hand radio. It could have been a grenade that she carried, hidden at her breast. Or the hopes of a continent. Or a rifle. Or god. Or a single flower, walking in the rain.

But time and the fates are fooled only in thought, and by these laws Amelia Fisher belonged forever to her own private downpour and she was not these women and she carried none of these things with her through the cold electric violence of that afternoon.

What she had come to carry always was the mild sickness of her life; the fevers that she fought so hard to hide away inside her ribcage these twenty-six years on earth. It was fever that danced her mother loose of this place. Fever whispered to Payne and spun him round in circles and made him a killer and filled his heart with the white coals of revolution and fever left him empty and he would never see the sky again.

Amelia would not let it take her hand. She had promises to keep.

When she reached the house she looked at the roof and saw the weathervane spinning and the water running sideways down the shingles, flooding the gutters. She walked up the porch steps and opened the door and came into the house.

She took off her shoes and walked into the kitchen and stood, tiptoe, in front of the high pantry. She felt with her hands and found what it was that she needed and brought the big soup pot, with the handles, down out of the pantry and filled it with water and lit the front burner and placed it there on the stovetop.

Then she walked over to the other side of the kitchen and pulled open the refrigerator door. She found celery and a bag of carrots in the bottom drawer and she took these things out and put them on the counter.

In the cupboard she found three big onions and she brought them down.

She went to where the knives were and chose the one with the widest blade and she took the wooden cutting board from where it hung on a nail and she set to dicing the vegetables.

When she was done she walked over to the stove and saw that the water was nearly boiling and she went back to the refrigerator and took out the whole chicken that her father had brought in the night before. It was wrapped in brown butcher paper and sealed with masking tape and she pulled the paper free and put the chicken into the water that boiled gently now in the soup pot. She lowered the flame to let it cook and brought herself upstairs to shower while it did.

She came down feeling good in her dry clothes and she took the chicken out and put it on a plate to cool and she brought the cutting board over to the stove and, holding it against the edge of the pot, pushed the vegetables into the water with the side of her hand.

After she had added the salt and pepper, the dried oregano and thyme, she leaned and reached for one of the big wooden spoons that lay on the shelf above the stove and she began to stir the simmering broth. The homemade smell of it filled the kitchen and found its way into the other quarters of the house and Amelia went to the cooked chicken and lifted it onto the cutting board and took up the same knife and began to cut the animal apart.

She separated the legs and thighs from the body and pulled the meat off the bone with her hands. It came easily. She took the knife and cut into the breast along the soft cartilage and pulled the white meat free and placed it down on the side of the cutting board, next to what she'd taken from the dark parts.

She used her hands to find all the rest of the smaller pieces that hid in the wings and under the body and in the rear.

Then she dumped the carcass and the bones into the garbage pail under the sink and returned to the cutting board and spread the meat out and cut it into pieces. She had kept the skin and she cut that up as well. Her father liked the skin.

Again she walked with the cutting board over to the stovetop, and holding it at an angle, pushed the meat into the soup and brought the cutting board to the sink and scrubbed it and rinsed it and dried it and hung it back on the nail against the wall. Then she did the same with the knife.

Returning to the stove, Amelia brought the heat down as low as the flame would allow without sputtering out and she stood over the soup and stirred it with the wooden spoon, watching the slow revolutions of the thing that she'd made, breathing it in.

It would be a little while before supper so she went into the living room and stood in front of the bookshelves. They had saved almost every National Geographic from a good part of the nineteen-eighties and two of the long bottom shelves were solely devoted to these magazines. She had read every one of them more than once but she liked the far away feeling they gave her, so she pulled one loose without looking at it and brought it with her over to the sofa and sat thumbing through the pages.

The female elephant will remember the precise location of drinkable water. She will travel great distances to return to that place. She could have been to the spring but once in her life, as a young calf, thirty or forty years in the past.

Amelia heard her father's truck pull up to the house. She rose from the sofa and slid the magazine back into its place on the bookshelf and she walked into the kitchen. The soup was done.

She turned the oven on and went to the cupboard and there she found the white flour and baking soda. She needed butter and milk and she got these from the refrigerator. Then she took down a stainless steel mixing bowl and began the batter and when it was done she got out a baking sheet and greased it and formed the biscuits and opened the oven door and put them in and she felt the heat touch her face as she did.

Her father had gone into the small barn by the house to put some tools away and he stayed there a little while to repair the cord on his power saw. When he came into the house he was met by the smell of the soup and the baking and he was happy to be out of the rain.

—Dad? Amelia called from the kitchen.

—Its me.

—Supper's ready. She was taking the biscuits out of the oven.

—You're an angel, he called, and he pulled his boots off and came walking into the kitchen with his socks on. —It's funny to think, that as the old stubborn owner and operator of a halfway decent farm, I'd still be going hungry at the end of the day if it wasn't for you.

Amelia reached for the ladle and poured the soup into two china bowls and she brought them to the table and sat down.

—I thought this might go good with the rain, she said.

A light steam came rolling off the soup and they talked awhile and ate together there in the kitchen.

—Something on your mind lately?

—No, she lied. —Why?

—You've just seemed a little...he searched, —...far away.

Amelia put her spoon down slow and lifted her hand and passed it through her hair.

—Maybe I've been lost a bit in this book I've been reading, she lied again and moved to change the subject: —Remember *A Light In The Attic?*

—Every damn night for close to four years. You wouldn't sleep unless we read it over and over. And you never got tired of it. We got to where we didn't really need the book anymore. But you made me turn the pages anyhow.

—Because it wasn't the same without the pictures, she remembered.

—That's right, he said. —The pictures.

Amelia closed her eyes and begged until she saw that honest little sketch of a child's face, it's brow an open window, and she begged on until the words came whispering back from wherever they lay in atrophy.

> *There's a light in the attic.*
> *Though the house is dark and shuttered,*
> *I can see a flickerin' flutter,*
> *And I know what it's about.*
> *There's a light on in the attic.*
> *I can see it from the outside,*
> *And I know you're on the inside...lookin' out.*

Now a hard wind came up, slaving the rain so that it rifled with new zeal against the house and the ground and her father turned his head and looked through the space between the curtains that half covered the pane window above the sink.

He nodded toward the weather and his eyes stayed a moment, fixed beyond the window glass.

—It's bad out there, said Paul Fisher.

10

The post office closed at noon on Saturdays. Amelia needed to mail an electric bill and buy a book of stamps so she asked Lilly if she could borrow her car. Lilly said sure and Amelia left her in charge of the stand and drove out into the clear late morning.

She rode with the windows down and the spring winds, as they came into the car, sent her hair tossing and the sheer movement of the vehicle felt so good underneath her body.

She pulled up in front of the small country post office and walked in through the glass doors, noticing the beaten mums that lined the walkway as she came, nearly ruined by Thursday's rains.

When she came in, there was no one else waiting for service so she went straight to the counter. She could hear Old Abbey and Garrison arguing in the back by where the mail was sorted.

—You better check again, Garrison was saying.

—He called four times. And he's a retired police officer. And a veteran.

—I don't care if he's Captain America, I'm sure there's nothing for him from Publishers Clearing House. Everything's been delivered today.

—And there was nothing yesterday?

—What does he think? Does he think he's a winner? What would he do with the money? No hooker would step foot in his house. And he's on oxygen anyway. Crazy old bastard. Does he think he can take it with him when he shits the bed for good?

—What did I tell you about that language in a public office?

Abbey should have retired three and half years ago and given her position as postmaster over to someone younger and more capable. She wet her pants on the job almost every day and nothing was ever in order and the only reason she was still there was because she had always been there and her higher-ups didn't know what to do about her and they were too embarrassed to ask her to go.

The mailman, Garrison, was a connoisseur of fine imported beers. He rode on his route with a cooler disguised as a letter basket resting in the back seat of his sorry Chrysler sedan. People got the wrong mail. Sometimes people got no mail. Garrison didn't care in the least. But he did have a vaguely noble feeling in his heart about the enduring legacy of his craft and he kept the code of the mail carrier stapled to his dashboard next to a picture of the Reverend Doctor Martin Luther King.

—Pardon me, said Amelia when she couldn't wait any longer.

They hadn't seen her come in and Abbey jumped when she spoke and came waddling up to the front where Amelia stood.

—Oh, Amelia. I didn't know you were

there. Garrison and I were just working out some bugs.

Garrison laughed.

—Hello, Garrison. Amelia waved to him where he stood in the back. She liked Garrison.

—Good day, Amelia.

—What can we do for you? Abbey broke in.

—I lost my checkbook and I need to mail this bill today so I'd like a money order for eighty-one seventy-four, please.

Abbey went to the money order machine and fumbled with it awhile.

—Eighty what?

—Eighty-one seventy-four, Garrison called from the back.

—No one asked you.

—So long, Amelia. Enjoy the weekend. Maybe I'll stop out at the stand. My mom's been hassling me for strawberries.

—You're not going anywhere, Mister, Abbey told him in her irate tone.

—I'll save the best for you, called Amelia.

—Thanks. He walked out the back door.

—Come back! Garrison!

They heard his car start up outside and drive away.

—What am I going to do with him? Abbey asked the money order machine.

—I also need a book of thirty-eight cent stamps when you're done there, said Amelia, cautiously.

Abbey didn't hear a word she said. Warm urine was running down her leg and she was thinking about the boardwalk at Atlantic City.

There were three cars parked at the stand when Amelia returned and as she came walking over she could see that Lilly looked distressed. She was adding someone's total and the pen had run out of ink and two other women were waiting to be rung up and one of them had a baby harnessed onto her back and the baby would not stop wailing.

A man was crouched down at one of the baskets and he was touching the fruit with his hands and asking rudely what day they were picked and what kind of fertilizer was used on their crops. It was all too much for Lilly and when she saw Amelia she was so relieved that she almost cried.

—Those were picked yesterday, Amelia said to the rude man. —We pick them fresh every other day. If you want to, you can pick them yourself. It's less expensive.

—I have a bleeding ulcer.

—I'm very sorry to hear that. What's the trouble, Lilly?

—My pen's run out of ink.

Amelia reached into the pockets of her jeans and she found the pen that she had forgotten to give back to Abbey at the post office. She handed it to Lilly. Then she started to put the things the women had on the counter into paper bags. The baby had stopped screaming and the crouching man got up and muttered something about bitches and drove away.

When everyone had left, Lilly leaned against the wooden counter and sighed.

—Wasn't that an ugly baby?

—Have you seen my father at all this afternoon?

—No. I haven't seen any of the boys. Usually someone comes to help if it gets busy.

—That wasn't busy.

—It felt busy.

Amelia smiled but she didn't say anything.

—How was your ride?

—It was fine, Lilly.

—Don't you just love driving?

It did get fairly busy later on in the afternoon and when the end of the day came both of them were very glad to see it.

Amelia told Lilly that it was all right if she wanted to leave a little early.

—I'll stay and help you close. You know I don't mind.

—Really, Lilly. You had a lot on your hands today.

—You sound like your dad. I'm staying here until we're all finished.

Amelia laughed. She hadn't seen her father all day and she began now to wonder why that was.

They put everything away and Lilly swept while Amelia counted the day's money. A breeze had come up.

—See you in the morning, Lilly.

—I might look a little scary.

—Are you planning on staying out late?

—It's Saturday.

—Well, have fun.

—Thanks, Amelia. You too.

Lilly drove off and Amelia was about to

leave when Sweet Walter showed up.

—I can't talk, Walter. I have to go find my dad.

Sweet Walter didn't seem to mind. He worked night hours at the bridge and he didn't sleep much and he never took anything that happened in the daylight too seriously.

—I'm sorry, she said.

He had the radio playing loud and he could barely hear what Amelia was saying. He was singing along with the Temptations and he kept on singing as he drove away.

Amelia ran down to the cow barn and asked Billy if he'd seen her father. He hadn't. Both tractors were in.

She was worried now and she ran back up past the stand and across the road and on up the driveway. There were brown puddles left by the rain and she stepped in them but she didn't know it. When she got close enough to see the house, she looked for her father's truck but it wasn't there in front where he always parked it.

She came into the house. She was breathing hard. It wasn't like him to disappear.

When her breathing had slowed, she began to feel the home surrounding her. She heard the quiet space and the quiet space held its own breath and swallowed its own kind of fear. Then she heard the sound of metal on metal. It came from the back yard.

She put her hands into the pockets of her jeans and found her legs to walk her through the house. She came onto the back porch. It wasn't dark yet but the sun was close to falling, and there she stood on the painted boards, looking out to where she could see her father's wiry body bent over and half hidden underneath the hood of the nineteen seventy-six Ford pickup truck that no one had touched in fourteen years. And the willow spread itself wide above the operation in the field, to shelter them both, sad man and sad engine.

—You sweet soul, she said in a dry choked whisper. —You sweet man.

Then she began to cry.

Paul Fisher reached into his toolbox and, replacing one thing, brought out another and went on working beneath the branches at his noticeably unhurried pace. His back was to the house and he had no notion of his daughter being there, watching him, tears rolling.

Amelia took her sleeve and dried her eyes and face on the fabric and went walking down the four porch steps, feeling the weakness in the old boards as she came, carrying herself out to her father.

—Shame on you, she said lightly as she reached the truck.

—Who? His hands kept on working and he didn't look up at her.

—You, she said. —I told you I'd do the work.

—Well, it's just about done.

She watched the steady turning of his farmer's wrist. The veins in it. The vein in his temple. The two freckles there.

—And this is where you've been all day.

—Here and in town. I went to the parts store for a few things. Plugs. A battery. And I stopped at the DMV on the way home and picked you up a pair of plates. You won't get far without those. Even around here. Not with all the road blocks these days.

He finished what he was doing and he returned the wrench and wiped his hands on a checkered rag that he pulled from his back pocket. He looked at her.

—I found a set of tires I'd forgot about behind some stuff in the barn. They're not new but the tread is halfway decent.

She hugged him and put her head against his chest.

—Thank you, Dad.

He held his arms out, the grease rag in one hand. He didn't want to soil her clothes; to soil her.

—This old bitch was in better shape than I would've ever guessed, he said.

11

The woman he loved was dead and he rolled out of their bed the same way every morning, rinsed his face and headed downstairs, his fisher's hands holding taut to the handrail as if it might be a long ago summer that he held or maybe a ladder to a different world.

Coffee wrecked his stomach so he drank black tea. The kettle was always on the stovetop, always poised to be manhandled, filled with tap water, set down above the gas flame to boil and scream. The spout steamed and he pulled his trusted cup from the drying rack beside the sink and found himself a tea bag and poured. Then he walked through the kitchen and out onto the big porch that faced the sea to face the morning.

The old boards gave softly under his feet as he came across the porch to the far left corner where the view was best and where, long ago, he had built a simple table of cut stone for them to be happy around, to talk simply or heavily, to look into the eyes of the other or out onto the water, careless in the mild seasons.

He sat, placed the tea down, laid his hands on the table and watched as a reckless gull flew alone above the beach. He watched the gull begin to lose its grip in the thousand moody winds that blow sometimes kind sometimes wicked along the coastline, both wings shivering in the pull like cold hands or scared hands and the man at the table knew what that could mean and the gull buckled further but would not be overcome, taking pains to fight for a hold on its buckling self until it found that hold and came to fly right again, as if just to fly was all that it would ever need.

He lifted his cup and blew on the surface to cool the tea and then he drank, warm going down, metallic on the gums. He looked again and the gull was gone. Gone like so many other beating hearts he'd known and where do they all go? I hope it's kind, he thought. Wherever they go, I hope it's kind. I hope the colors are good.

Colors had come to mean so much more to him after he'd lost the last of his hearing for keeps and a change in the sea could make him young again or a change in the sea could break his back or make him sing. He could fall asleep on the dock and wake up under a wholly different sky and the colors in that sky could tell him to live forever or they could scream down leave this world for good.

Where would we go? he thought. I hope we leave our meanness at the door. Our frailty at the door and the colors are kind and the ground is soft and there are no flies to bite us.

Sometimes they would talk all night, John Sparrow and his black-haired love. For at that time he could still hear some things but only faintly as if through a wall and so in this injured way these two would speak far into their nights, pausing to see fall the blazing casualties of the sky fleeing heaven like running refugees running for a place to belong while back down on a forever divided earth the waves rolled in and rolled away, off to find other wishful patterns and other injured lovers by the sea.

—What will you do when I'm gone?
—I'll get on all right.
—Will you?
—I don't like to think about it, he said, staring out past the railing.
She wanted him to say that he'd die without her but she knew he wouldn't. He'd go on living more or less the way he had before they met. He'd fish. He'd turn again to shadowboxing his memories and she would be just one more thing for him to fight in the dark. She pitied her aging soldier, his wars turned inward now.
—You need to know something before I die, she said.
He took a long breath in. Tired. Tired of all the dying.
—They said you could live another five six years.
—They say a lot of things. I'm already dead, lover. I've been dead awhile.
—What about the time we've had?
—Borrowed, at best. Naive. She looked at him and touched his face. —Beautiful. She began to cry. —Breathless. Unbearable. I never thought I could love.
—You've loved me. Loved me well.
—Yes I have, darling. Loved you like a drug. Like the end of the world.
They held each other there on the rocky brink of a continent. He listened to her breathing. Shallow. Difficult. She coughed. Coughed again.

—Remember how we used to sing Blackbird? he asked.

—I need to tell you something. You have to know...

—I know a lot of things I'd like to forget. Right now I want to know about Blackbird. How we'd lie out on the ground with the reeds all around us. The wind through them knocking the time. And us singing. I think we've done alright with broken wings.

—I have a daughter, John.

This he heard. The night heard. It listened and waited with him in the singing quiet.

—Oh God...a daughter. Black hair like mine. Lovelier than me. Four years old. She was four years old when I ran. Rose Marie looked out to the water. *—Eyes that could swallow up the world. She looked into me. No one ever did that. I couldn't bear it. Not from her.*

John Sparrow took her frail waist and drew her close but she was somewhere else.

—I'm sorry I kept it from you.

—Do you think it would have changed a thing? We're every one of us living with shadows.

—I thought you'd think me cruel. I was so cruel.

—Rose, in three years I burned alive more souls than I would ever try to count. Maybe half of them were grown men. I saw the bodies. The little ones with them, half sheltered under them. Jesus, the smell. We blackened a part of the world. Not the first time and certainly not the last. It was hell on earth. And I was on hell's side. I know that now.

—You were young.

Goodbye, Amelia.

—And so were you, he said. —Every one of us was young. I was deceived.

—I think I might have been, too.

—Deceived?

—Kept in the dark. They told me nothing about my body. Less about my heart. How could I carry a separate life in my gut? I couldn't carry my own. The woman breathed. —She tore me apart, that little girl. They had to sew me up. That bloody little girl.

They held each other now and neither of them spoke, both knowing after this long that words can be nothing but poison and the past just a salesman.

Far far out, they could see the lights of a fishingboat trembling silver yellow on the black horizon, searching on through the pretty malaise of those hours.

—She'll come here, John.

—What?

—She'll come looking for me and I'll be dead.

—How could you know?

Rose Marie said nothing. She was following the boat lamps fading fading fading away into the gone.

—Promise me you'll love her when she comes. Hold her. Walk with her on our beach. Sit, the two of you, at this goddamned table and don't you let her go.

She pulled her head away from the night and looked into his face.

—Will you let her know I was green? That I was so lost and green.

—I'll do my best, Rose.

He watched her eyes, eyes like a city on fire. Fire sets us on our own, makes us warm awhile, steals our breath away.

—I was petrified, she said, the whole of her somewhere else. —Petrified.

Aren't we all, thought John Sparrow.

—And, John.

—Yes, Rose.

She quaked.

—Tell her I said goodbye.

12

This night she slept and the good part of her sleep was filled with the robin egg blue stillness of not dreaming. Then she did dream. Dream a red sky. Red as Mars. Bring the war, Mars. Red like one day when the wrists of heaven lay open wide and all of its spies have come from out of the corners to open theirs as well.

Under this sky is where Amelia stands, lost in her body. Shivering naked upon an empty runway. Look at the airfield. Abandon. Its people have run run run run away to leave the whole thing orphaned and whispering on into debris and no right angel would bring itself to stand inside the perimeter, let alone spread its wings, beat the dust from them.

A pear tree has grown up out of a wound in the runway, a hundred yards ahead of where she stands. A woman is there with the tree, her back to Amelia. She is twisting a pear free, taking it down. Rose Marie.

Amelia can see what remains of the air traffic control tower, see it where it rises up in its atrophied pose from out of the blacktop earth and all of its windows have passed away but not the desperate waiting that was done through them on ten thousand dirty golden afternoons, waiting for the far hum, the approach, the agony of landing gear, and finally the hush. Bring them in alive, don't let them burn up, they are boys.

A man has come to stand in the space where the wide windows had been, a shrouded form erect in the high haze and light about the tower. He is searching. Like a new widow on the beach, unwilling to give her tall fisher over to the sea. Her beloved to the sea. Eyes peeled for signs. Signs that will not come.

And so this man has passed his internment by hunting the wide bloodscape; hunting for liberty and chaos and beauty and time and now he weeps forever at what it is that he's found. He is the searcher the lover the killer the thief the prisoner the child of the morning sun and his place is in the tower and now from the tower he turns his weeping head down to naked Amelia and here is the face of Payne; turned old and battered but lovely still like the frail ghost of a dandelion waiting on in limbo after the spring, sear and tired and happy as hell to be blown away.

Payne calls out to her; calls down through the red dream: —Could you inherit the weight? he asks, all the wilderness gone out of his voice. —The weight of the wind? Will you, my love? Will you inherit the weight of the wind?

Having said his piece, he turns and moves back into the shadows of the control tower.

Having listened, Amelia turns her head to look upon the runway and the pear tree and the reaping woman one last time. But the tree is bare. The woman is gone.

Rose Marie. Just out of reach.

Goodbye, Amelia.

Amelia woke beneath the blankets. She threw them from her, reached for the string and pulled the light bulb on in her room. Standing up, she spied a pair of jeans on the hardwood floor. She got into them and took a light sweater from off her desk chair and pulled it on. She went into her closet and into her drawers and took things out and put them all into an army duffel bag, threadbare and well loved, gone with her everywhere. She hunted and found her dying camera exiled away inside a shoebox. She pulled it free.

She crossed the hall and touched lightly her father's bedroom door. It opened and in she came to stand with the darkness above his bed. He looks like a boy, she thought. A child. Is that what we are?

She knelt and kissed his sleeping face.

He stirred.

—What's happening? the child asked his daughter without truly waking.

—There's a light on in the attic, she said, half insane to suffer the pull.

—What's that you say?

—I've lost something, Dad, she said. —Something that should never be lost. Her voice breaking like a thin vow. —I love you, Dad. She touched his hand and turned away. —But I have to get it back, she said into the dark. —What would I be without it?

She inhaled and left the room.

In the kitchen she poured a glass of water, drank it down and left it by the sink.

Outside in the dark she felt the cold dew all around her with the morning far away.

Climbing into the truck, finding the key on the dashboard, closing the heavy door as lightly as she could, bringing the newly healed machine to life with a turn of the ignition, Amelia drove out to the road and away from all that she knew.

Nearly an hour later, the highway making its easy ascent, she came to the top of the rise and looked down onto the wide darkened river and the proud bridge that spanned it with its odd lights out of place above the water and as she drove down to the bridge-crossing there were no other cars and she felt clear, ready to live and no one could take that away. Not this morning.

Sweet Walter was in his box and when she pulled up alongside he smiled his true smile and Amelia could see the lines in the skin that bordered his eyes, lines of laughter and heartache and sleep lost, beaten and beautiful somehow, poorly famed in the untrue tollbooth light.

—You are a sight to see, he told her.

—I'm leaving, Walter.

—And where will you go? There was no surprise in his voice. No pretense. Love alone.

—I've got to find her.

—Goodbye, Amelia, he said through his smile but it was a different smile now.

—Goodbye, Sweet Walter.

She drove out onto the bridge and he watched her go. The taillights go.

—Find who, child? he asked out past the toll window into what little remained of the night. —Who will you find?

Amelia held tight to the steering wheel, tight to the strange providence of the open world. And far under the bridge below her the black river water churned and churned over to the call of its own sleepless longing, its own orphaned cry for the sea. Starved for the cradle of the sea. Scared to death to know that in the end it might come only to find some wild echo of its own awful face grinning back at it, hungry and lost somewhere behind the fever-colored windows of the sea.

And who could hope to quiet the flux?

Run river run.

Run daughter run.

Book Two

Prayers of the
Silver Propeller
A Collection

Book Two
Prayers of the Silver Propeller
A Collection

Prayers of the Silver Propeller

Another was born to the world today. Born into the air. A light rain coming over the mountain and down on the land to baptize soft the act. The mother is stiff but the stiffness is mended quick by the remedies of her blood and by the long purple gravity of the sky overhead, the sundown sky. The babe trembles in the failing light. And though it cannot see the high dying clouds above, it knows them. Knows that its shape had shone in them before this day and will again, called by the brief brief turnings of the high wind. There will be milk in this new darkening world of the babe and with the milk will come the finding of its own secular pulse from out of the roar of all the beating hearts upon the prison earth.

The elephants move in country. They move on in company, the same as other beasts, but something else moves with them, beside them. Shadows. A sadness under the skin. Skin like the hard blinds of history. Lasting skin like the canvas of tents. Skin without a home like the far origin of night. Skin like the blanket of night. One of their number carries a wound in its side the shape of a field sickle. He is a grown male who came to breed and leave but was maimed and taken in. It hurts but it heals. The others would not leave him; they set a new pace and sung from the gut. Songs of hope to push him through. It was not his time. He gets on better than yesterday and tomorrow will be easier still. The sky is still. The sorry little body of water where they've stopped to drink had been still for days before the surface was broken open by the thirst. He stands and they rinse the crescent wound; water falling off his side to soften the greed of the thirsty land. The land drinks it up. Men drink other things. It was men who put the sickle to his side.

And this time of year the flocks come rifling through the high passes. Five hundred and more running the air on until it suits the blood. And in the air they do become each other and trade souls like hats. One sidelong glance and they change change change change change as they fly. Amnesia hasn't found her way into these birds yet and so they carry the knowing that nothing belongs to itself. Latitude lines are under them but these hearts pound holier than the lines. Hearts that pound with fever that the draftsman of the lines traded away for ceilings and empty prayers. Prayers of things you can touch. Prayers of coins. Prayers of bricks. Prayers of the silver propeller. But who will pray for the unbearable lightness of nudity and empty hands? The way the birds go is set down by the fevers of the sky and by their screeching and by the screeching unity of their souls. There was a time when some would break from the exodus to light down onto the backs of the elephants, but not today. A rift has come between them. A rift where there was none. And one pays no mind to the other as they cross.

He loves her dearly but she doesn't know. She had given birth once before but the calf had come out dead. He was there and watched as her body heaved to push it loose and was moved to see no strain in her face and afterward he was moved and curious to see her turn and stride away from the thing, there lifeless and bad and gray, staining the dry earth and the blond grasses of the plain. This mother knew too well that the babe had come undone inside her and she didn't have to look at it to see. He stayed. Stayed after the others had moved on, unable to take his eyes from it. Pregnancy to him was a thing of rumor. A red whisper in a place like night. A whisper that he'd never catch the whole of. He was made for different pains, this one.

He can see her up ahead, her son walking with very little grace beside her. He sees that the swelling in her backside has gone down. The smell that is hers alone does not fail to find its way against the skin of his face and rest there like an aching veil to be torn away by the mean winds of afternoon. A half-sweet smell like dying or like flowers that can't exist anymore but did when the land was young and its musks had no bridle.

Did I invite this wound of mine so they would keep me on a little longer? Until the wound, she had never brushed against me. I think she didn't know I lived before the wound. All her life I've known her and have noted her growth at intervals. Her father was a great one in his time. He died bad to lighten the circumstance of his kind. His blood is hers and it is that which I call for in the silence and from the darkness of my hollow gut but she does not know my need because my calls are lost in my fear of being close to another. Others run away. Others die and change. Others lose what they had when you saw them first in the goldish haze of morning. Others change and leave memory to die a liar and a thief. But this one with the new child is different. One brush against her has been worth all the pain of living but tomorrow I will go away alone.

The father of the babe had been killed by killers on the plain not an hour after they'd finished mating. She wept in her own way but the killing did not seem serious to her. She watched him fall onto his side from a good distance away but she felt even further away. The brush and spare trees on the hills stood to serve as a filter for her sentiment. She watched him kick and flail until he kicked and flailed no more and as she turned away she knew that most of her life was full of not feeling. Him dying there in the open gave her the same far away nausea as when he left his seed in her belly. He had twitched and grunted the same as when he died and he bled there in the open the same as she would bleed and the same as all the world would for life and sex and dying. She feels her father now in the babe as it struggles to find its feet and it won't be long before its back is higher than hers and its eyes are rimmed with the hard light of searching, set to the horizon with all the blue sadness and patience of the turning skyway.

All the next day a warmth lay over the land and storm clouds shone on the western edges but it did not rain until the sun came well past its highest point and was lost as the clouds spread high and wide. The elephants watched the rain fall far ahead in the air and on the distant ground a long time before it came down on them and when it did come it was light and not cold and they were glad for it.

They came to a place where the grasses grew waist high. The rains had passed and the sun was setting where it does and here the band came suddenly upon the rotting body of a turned-over pickup truck. They stopped, one and all. The tires came up over the grass and faced the sky, flat and cracked and sad-looking. The axles and undercarriage lay rusting on. The elephants stood and took in the fine details of the thing before them. Passenger window gone. A radio antenna bent to another shape. The webbed break in the front window glass like the wild patterns in the eyes of some. The bleached paint of the truck body and the different shades to be found in it. The air turned clear and cool in the dying light and the weep-for-living smell of dusk after rain was all about them but it did not hide what smells lingered on the truck and would not leave the seats. The animals moved on, keeping distance. They knew that smell.

If they had passed this way in the light of another dusk four years gone they would have seen the same truck racing across the plain. They would have seen the big jeep following it. Hunting it. The driver of the truck pulling hard on the wheel in a last hope to turn off toward the mountain road. The soil failing the worn tires and the pickup truck rolling over many times until it came to rest bottom up with the engine smoking and leaking different things into the ground. Who sought peace inside the truck now struggled to be out. The driver, a boy fourteen. The other, his sister eleven. Men in the jeep behind them had shot and killed their father in the same hour as he knelt working in the garden outside the shack where the family lived. Their father spoke out against the coming tide of bad new law. He tried to give what little he had to those with less and spoke out and spoke out and this is why he died. The children had kicked the passenger side window free and climbed out and lay panting and broken in the soil as the jeep pulled beside them. A man stepped out and he carried a rifle with him and he carried what weighed more but cannot be seen. The girl had liked colored string and the way it felt when you pulled it tight between your hands. The boy wanted to fly planes.

In the night the elephants slept close. The smell and the picture of the dead truck would not leave the babe and he shivered and slept bad against the bulk of his mother. It would never leave him, nothing would, and he might come to know this with time. His young breath, sweet as it came to blend with the night air and go away, carried trouble on it and this woke the mother but as she looked to her side she saw that the trouble was within him and that she must leave her son to the pains of memory if he were to make it through this life. She looked now at the others sleeping round her and saw there a tiredness that was past resting. She saw a faint seizure that rippled through an ear and then went back into the calm and to the chaos of night. She saw tails twitch and backs twitch and she saw a chest settle strange. Could they not be free from the lonesome toil of all these clear dreams that own? No. They suffer the throes of night and have for sixty million years on this blue earth. She took her eyes from them and turned to find the charcoal sky.

Was it always this way? she thought. So empty with its cold lights burning. Could it ever come tumbling down?

She felt a wave of pity go through her. Pity she had not known. For herself and for her son and for all who bore their shape, now or ever. She did not sleep again and when the morning shone copper and unreal in the new sky the others woke easily and the band moved on across the plain.

In the shade of trees they rested and ate what grew there on the ground. Three of the young had taken up a kind of game and a fourth came to join and together they rolled small logs between them and they were happy in the cool forest light. Insects circled and passed over and under the grazing band and some landed and stayed and left and circled again and if the elephants cared they did not show it. The small grove of trees above and all around them offered up smells that are not found in the open lands. Sap and blossom and good soils that lie free from the merciless scrutiny of the sun, and different smells that are older and faint and stifle even the very air they ride on. Spare pools of rainwater endured and they lowered their trunks like dry hands to drink. The water tasted clean and cool and the feel of it took their breath away and this night the dreams ran lighter.

Raw dawn found them pressing through the open mist, and the grasslands shrouded as they were began to take on form and it was all made real as the hungry sun rose like a red beggar up from the lost fringes of the world and high above the morning a single warplane tore through the aching fascia of the stratosphere. Elephants know the engine. Engines roar in every corner of the earth where men have breathed a life into all their angry infant things that hum and grind and spit and through folly and circumstance men have lost the right to take that life away and so these things roar on and will. The pilot flew alone in the sad green jumpsuit of his trade. For all the stars against his chest he flew alone. Under the helmet his hair was cut short and most of it had gone to silver with the passing days of his life. His name was Byrd and he sat harnessed into the ejector seat thinking about a girl he hadn't seen in thirty-seven years.

He thought of the time he rode with her late in the day out past the far edges of town to where the road turned rough and on until it was only them out there. It was the end of summer and this was all new to him. The foreign smell of her, the words she used. Someone had told her about the place they here going to, about how from this one field, at the right part of night, the stars were like nothing else. Lying there with her, after turning off the car and walking out into the high grass, he felt as though he shouldn't have come. She held his hand and told him how she felt about living. He listened. His back was cool against the ground though he couldn't stop the sweating and the sky above them burned on. She told him that it was hard for her to believe in anything. Then she told him that she did believe in some things, but she wouldn't tell him what. He didn't see much of her after that. He joined early in the Navy and they went around the world on boats but he never saw much of it, only the ports and the ports were no more than half real. Most everyone seemed drunk or desperate in some way. People sold things. Girls sold their own bodies. Back out on the water it was easier for him. He saw so many different birds. He saw a man drown and it stayed with him. They lived long on the ocean. Small on the ocean. The sailor in the bed closest to him would cry himself to sleep most nights. He would lie awake long after the breathing of the sailor was still and wonder what it was that could break a man that way, the both of them no more than nineteen years old.

A voice came barking over the radio in the cockpit and he told the voice what it wanted to hear and then he reached and turned the radio off.

He thought about being young at home. The Christmas when there was no money and his mother had made them gifts so they wouldn't have to go without. She had sewn together a pillow for him with her hands. A thing to place between her son and the world. He had complained about the pillow, had wanted something out of the catalogue. Their father hadn't been in the house for three years but they could feel him there. Walking down the upstairs hall that night on his way to bed he saw the bathroom door open a little way; that part of the house that smelled like soap and paint and always had. He stopped and in the light beyond the door space he could see their old mirror hanging in long witness to all things that had passed in that bathroom and it will never tell. There, the crown of his mother's head reflected in the glass, crying into her hands, the dirty golden light from the lamp. He thought that it might be him she was crying over and this gave him value. But it wasn't him. This mother of his cried that hour because to her it was yesterday that she was gathering late flowers in the cool halflight before bed in a September lost. No light hair and no needs at all yet between her legs and now here were the gathering lines in her face and the gathering clouds behind her eyes and where was all the time between? How could she touch it? He watched and listened for awhile, then he turned his head away, on to the bed where he had slept his small life long, his feet going quieter than they had come.

I bet the house is gone, Byrd said out loud and the sound of it hung strange in the lost oxygen of the cockpit and he looked at all the lights and the switches and buttons and triggers that he knew the feel of better than he knew the woman who carried and nursed him. Better than he knew any woman. Anyone. I bet it's gone, he said again and reached to turn the radio back on and as he did he saw by the gauges that his course had strayed and that his fuel had run terribly low. He reached now and pulled hard against the wind and he turned the craft around in the cold fear of losing his way and there in the asthma of panic he fought to wrest himself free from the other Byrd whose lips were chalk and whose cries rang out like a siren in the cockpit and whose face hung stolen by a hungrier year and whose true life lay atrophied and lost within the quilted lies of altitude and time and when he thought he had a hold on it he called down to the airbase and told the other servicemen that he was coming home.

The Boy and the Barrel

Down by his grandfather's house there is a barrel for burning. It's been a good way to get rid of papers, dead envelopes and magazines. Lone is the condition of the barrel, there behind the old barn and it could never be another way. When he would come to it with a basket of papers he imagined he could feel the barrel needing what was in his hands, as he sometimes needed things. He felt like it knew him, trusted him, but he never told this to anyone, of course.

The basement of his grandfather's house was low and different. It took a while for the lights to come on after you turned the switch at the stairtop. They would flicker and die then come on low then come on right. He never knew any other lights like that.

When the fire was in the barrel he would stand above it and turn it with a stick, which at all other times rested against the barn wall. That stick was a part of the same thing that the barrel was, charred and changed by the years. It belonged to the barrel. The fire did not belong to the barrel. The fire was free or if not free it belonged to another fire that was far away.

His grandmother would watch him burning from where she sat on the porch. He

thought she watched because she was proud
that he was big enough now to do it by himself;
proud of the good job he did with the papers. No,
it was fear that had her watching. He waved and
stirred the bottom and big ashes lifted
themselves out and rode on with the breezes in
the yard.

Yesterday

The insects are larger, more confident.

A naked moron is pissing—one of the first men that ever there were.

Something bigger than him will come before long from out of the shadows—thirsty to hunt him down—tear him apart—drawn by the smell.

The change has been little.

It smelled more or less the same yesterday against the toilet in the Men's Room opposite the War Room inside the District of Columbia. But what is yesterday? Where is it?

Simone Felice

Amnesty from the Fingers

I was small but you were small once too, old
man. And from a boy I have feared your
warheads. Rumors from the car radio. Three feet
tall in the backseat not knowing what it is that
the voice says but being cold and afraid all the
same. Rumors at the dinner table. Rumors from
the television. Your newsman in his bad shirt.
His bad face. And when we witness this
compound word over and again so many times
we become so afraid of it, so very afraid of it.

Warheads. Warheads.

But it is no modern thing. No new fear native or
significant to the last century or to the embryo of
this one. It is in fact a thing as definite and
residual as blood and bone because you and
your sort of men have always been born with
war heads.

You have had more than one name, old man.
And you have indeed been with us here since the
very hour when the first tools were made.

But where was it that you learned how to tie so
fine for it to be without our ever knowing that

115

you have tied us all up into little knots? Tying and tying without rest. Without ever resting. With your hearsay always on the wind, in the pamphlets, and now on the wires like some secret virus for which there is no immunity but which is itself immune to time.

But I have been untying. And I am free now, old man. And please don't believe that I am the only one.

I've seen your hydrogen bomb hiding in the tall grass and crying like a baby in the shadows behind the aeroplane hanger where she's lived since she was born.

—How could they shape me this way and put what they put inside of me?

She is asking this of the setting sun. Somehow knowing them to be one, these two. Made of a common thing, fire and whatever else. A puddle of her own urine now all but absorbed by the soil underneath her body.

—Why have they always been so afraid of themselves? Afraid of one another? These men touch me and touch me in a bad way. I have wished all my life for nothing more than amnesty from the fingers.

Before the Hour is Out

I feel the tape against my skin and the damp heat of it there. It has a hold on all the small hairs that no one will see again.

Before the hour is out I will have walked in through the door of the station with the dynamite taped down all along my belly and waist.

I will miss my mother when I go. She gave half her life to make sure I could breathe.

I will blow the better half of the building away, and my body too, but I will have taken eight of their number with me. It will hurt to ride the wind with my soul tied up in theirs but this is the pain that follows freedom and I will cry the same copper tears as my enemies as we are vacuumed away because we are all lost children when we leave our skin; screaming as we go, like so many helicopter blades, down and down and down.

A Brief Debriefing

Come with us.

We know who god is and we know who you are and who you've been.

This is your costuniform.

Take it and put it on.

The one who was dressed in it before you has been lost.

He had been shaped like you.

It should fit.

Church and Grenades

Grenades: If you find the shrapnel in her side, take it out. Please pull it out and stay with her through the spells. The door was a door until it gave with the blasting away. It's been a red year and she knows it with the sun down. It comes over me, she says. Over me.

Church: Do they know each other? Do they know who made their clothes? Will they drop their dollars like they've done so long? Will they sleep well? Will they know it when their time shows?

Grenades: Put the tourniquet away. Touch round the perimeter. Kiss the perimeter. You will be gone before daybreak and she will be gone too. Hold what's left of her against what's left of you. Let the loveless debris rain down against your tiny earth and pray hard you were a different animal.

I'd Love to Pull You Out of the Scenery

I'd love to pull you out of the scenery. Touch your hair. Be as close as we can. Forget all about the torpedoes.

But before any of that can come true I think I need to lie here balled up on the floor for another week with no one to change my pants, no one to rinse this body of mine.

A Time for Going

It looked like her but it wasn't. She left not long before we all watched the city on fire; some place in Israel she was going to. I can't remember the name but I remember how her eyes looked when she told me she was going. She knew something in her blood had her running and she told this to me too; that something in her blood had to be there. She'd heard that the sun lay across the old old land with a different sentiment entire in that gold and bitter place and she had to be under it. The ends of August have been a time for going, an early twilight with the world in an easy way, but there is no going without something other holding fast. I hope she's still alive. I hope she's found the sky the way she thought it would be.

Shame on the Boeings

See how these wrong clouds would feign a place among the true ones.

Shame on the Boeings of the world.

Shame on how their linear discharge lingers here in its sickly hover long after the aeroplanes have come and gone away.

Like some cursed highway whose end can only be found in the million crazed destinations of man and one day in his one destiny.

See its crafty shape laid here alongside these flawless billows who have been the non-denominational pilgrims of the always changing sky.

This derelict form in apparent company with the clouds; a sly remake not sly enough in its offwhite.

No different from the turned completion on the deadman. Deadman come to pose in his gentleman's finery. Pose in the midst of the living and the young.

This Blind Parallel

Men made out of cardboard and newspaper are the new sort of men and they burn oh they burn. Inside the epicenter of their hearts is found a great love and there too we find a great and palsied terror. The matchbook. So that the image of this one thing is to them both a Christ and a Shadowchrist.

And within this blind parallel they live and in that living witness all around them their contemporaries burning and calling out for water. And those not burning will not provide water but instead will clasp their hands tight together and bow those paper heads in the outward gesture of prayer and praying for the sweet mercy of the matchbook and all matchbooks.

Because still somewhere captive and tied to the intestines of these people is an inert and curious worship of that selfsame fire which by and by will certainly come to take them all from the world.

That Fabric Anatomy

Hitler had been an infant at one time.

He was at the nipple and so were we all.

He held the small patchwork animals soft between his hands and pressed them against his heart and so did we all.

With his eyes he could see and with those sapling fingers he could feel the sutures in that fabric anatomy, not unlike the boundaries that separate the nations of the world. The borders.

And they change. And they change. And they change.

Those lines which exist only on the inside of men's heads.

Does the wind know them?

Does the rain?

Out on the Beachscape

Out on the beachscape he is walking barefoot back from where he had been collecting shells and pieces of things that had been alive in another time.

Those small and delicate artifacts that the tides bring in. That the tides take away.

This expatriate talking freely with the sand, the sea, the night. The night coming from beyond the water as the very sun is pulled down past that changeless perimeter like a crayon sun by who knows what and will it show its face again?

Am I made from the same thing as those men?

Am I?

The same clay?

The same clay?

Dead Girl

She is a dead girl but she is not yet altogether gone away.

A queer light in the window.

A wind through the camouflage; a wind through me.

I never would have known about the monsters out there if she hadn't done the telling.

All the Turning

He made a wheel.

A thing born of love and mayhem both; an origin for all the turning.

Born of him, without knowing the feel of the dark blood between his legs but not without knowing the absolute pull of other blood and future future.

She made the rain come down.

Some things grew and some things drowned, but it was all the same.

The Peasant Has No Face

And we come only to find out time and again that the peasant has no face in this world and with no face there can be no claim to the physical things inside the world. No claim and in turn no real allegiance to any bishop or to any bureau but only to the very heart that moves the blood inside his body. Her body. And what moves that gorgeous organ can only be the same anonymous centrifuge that has always moved the birds of the sky. The thousand cattails by the roadside.

She's Been Running

She has somehow set this thing into motion and it has become what she's been running from even before she felt the infant revelation which tells us that these strange feet are in fact our own and she has always had split-second dreams of a postage stamp.

Dreams of an ant farm.

Dreams of an aeroplane.

Dreams of a firing line.

Dreams of an apple tree.

Dreams of her own body turned inside out by a force too transient and prehistoric to have any name at all.

Between Ourselves and Love

1. No mention of color.

She took his hand and led him on to the other side of the wall. A light played against her cheeks and a burning lived in his until the both of them passed from sight.

What they share is between them, the young, but what they carry away is not for the other to know.

She carried away the one she loved and it wasn't him. He tried to carry what he could of her: hair—her white legs, long and troubled—her troubled breathing.

The pieces of her underneath or beside his body, these will be with him through his life or until he falls from the weight and she will never pause to remember his name.

2. Yellow.

There are animals behind the yellow wall, mattresses too. The dog takes the hand of god and this is where they lie until all the lights of morning come pouring down upon their naked souls.

They sing out against the raw hour, this pair, sing out loud of the hushed love between them. Their song coming heavier than the light on their bed—heavier than the need of the dead on the outside—prettier than the living who hold to that life until their fingernails are gone.

3. Faded blue.

He walked through the opening in the faded blue wall and on down the path past a mailbox and past a child and on past a garden dying with the winter.

On up a small flight of stairs, his ears ringing as he pushed through the door at the top of the landing and made his way down the hall past the smells of people and carpet and on into the room where his mother was born. He sat on the bed. She was screaming in the mucus and he was nowhere that day.

He sat for a long time, touching the cheap blanket under him, wishing for a life of intrigue. The room needed painting. He stayed well into the night, waiting for what he couldn't touch.

4.Purple dark.

She made love to him outside. A path where mosses grew at the edge and no walkers anymore and this is how they lay. One last time she took him in against the purple dark of her walls. Weight on them both but each weight dumb to the other.

Will we ever find a common frailty in the sexes, a common temperature in the sex? She had carried a child and brought it into the air between here and the last time they'd touched. Its father was in another part of the country dying as they lay together in their faint way in the faint moisture of the thing they'd just done.

5. Again, no color.

She killed a man on the highway. The figure of the man had flailed, crazy in the road ahead and she was driving as fast as she could through the night, running away, as she had run before. She didn't once touch the brakes.

In the morning she woke alone to the sound of dirty love, a riot of springs and low cries through the thin wall of the motel where she'd spent the night. She had fallen asleep with the light on and now two moths circled and landed and circled and landed on and around the bulb, fighting or courting or both.

6. Red.

I am lost behind the red wall. My sweater is on the floor, cast away to let the winds of limbo rifle free through my skeleton. I've been in love. I've been inside a submarine.

7. White.

—Will I see you again?
—I can't say.
—You can't or you won't?
—Somewhere between.

—I saw your name on the white wall, oh darling I know what that means.

—There were other names besides mine.

—Don't try to make it better, hold on to me.

He held her close.

—They'll come and take you away.

—No, he lied, they never will.

—I know what they'll do. It's terrible. Terrible what they do.

—Quiet, love.

—And we never drove to the sea like we said we would.

—Quiet. We'll go, he lied.

—Tell me the truth.

—We'll take the car. It's such a nice drive along the coast. We'll lie in the sand and watch the sky together.

—What else, darling?

—We'll laugh out loud and think of a different time and talk about living free. We'll follow the sun and make love in the colors as it goes down.

Out the Train Window

For a long while there had been a highway running parallel to this railroad and alongside the highway the million telephone poles that have from day one promised always to keep us in touch but have they kept us in touch?

I can see farmland.

Now with the highway gone, the poles for the most part gone, everything I see is farmland and with it the living backdrop of the sky.

Now through the slightly dirty and moving frame that is the train window I am able to view, not far off, a small house and on the lawn is someone's daughter bringing down laundry from a clothesline. At this distance one could never see the clothespins but one knows them to be there between her fingers just the same.

Her movements are soft. Deliberate. Like those of someone who has walked a long time alone in the woods and has become aware to the notion that there is in fact a living world outside the manmade one. She folds the random textiles and lets them fall into the basket at her feet.

How would it be to fall in love with that girl and exist out here in the interior? To listen for the train at intervals and then watch it pass. A thing that should seem so wholly alien out in this place but does not. Its whistle and the riot of its coming and going common in the night. Outside. Herself and myself underneath this quilt. Inside. My farmgirl fast asleep against me. Her body smelling as authentic as a body can. The sound of her breathing in the bedroom being the most beautiful metronome the worldwide. I am not asleep. The train is passing. It comes and it goes away. The train is passing out there on the flats but I am coupled here with my love. It will not take me away never take me away with its promise of soon delivering its living cargo somewhere but in the end delivering it nowhere. She is breathing in the bedroom and I am not. No, she is outside in the last light of the day taking everything down from the clothesline and I am on the train seat half a mile away and half delirious watching her figure and the figure of the house grow small and small and she has no idea who I am.

Out the train window we are witness only to whatever truths the Americascape might be willing to share with us. All of her beautiful or maybe terrible algebra which lives and has lived in every tree, under all the rivers and inside every bird's stomach long before the boats came. So long before we plugged everything into the wall. But since this all has come to pass it would be unfair to say that her algebra has not been subsequently modified. Modified forever.

———

To wake in another part of the country without ever moving one's feet seems to me a felony against the very way we've been made.

I suppose I dreamt and in that dream I heard, more than once, my own self crying out for mercy from a thousand miles away. And though I could not see this twin otherself long across that dark expanse of land I knew that it was naked and tied to a chair. I knew also that the screamer was me and not me but some secret refugee come smuggled out of my mother's belly in the same minute as me and once this far lifeform had been young and once it had been free but at one time so had we all.

The sun has begun its rising through the darkness outside my window. Showing itself in its slight and tested way like a thin virgin standing inside of her thin slip against the bedroom door. Half of her visible, half of her lost, wishing not to reveal too much of what she is at once and so too has it always been with this same speculate wonder that men have waited for the coming of the sun.

Now in the half light there on the grasslands I am moved, in a way, to see rising out of the ground what I know not to be dinosaurs, of course, but here in this small and palsied hour of the morning their goliath shapes seem to own all the look of those animals and animalbirds who had long before any Eden been the sovereigns of this earth until whatever it was that took them away took them away.

But what I see out there in silhouette are no dinosaurs. The train and me inside the train are beginning to pass them now and I can see them for what they are. What the oilmen call the pumpjacks. The oilfields. See them. Down and up and down and up again, halfliving in their limited animé. Lonesome idiot heads, bobbing monstrous against the red sky behind. Pledged to one thing: the harvest of all fossils and fuel from out of that hard uterus under the world.

And I can see it as no light irony that these machines might have come to be shaped this way. Chance replicas of the very animal whose bones and sap have been stolen by this empire to make this empire what it is. And it is yet to be seen if the oilman and all his people might one day suffer the same end or perhaps a sister end. With these dead bones of ours as the chief component in a new and golden fuel made light and thin to propel god knows what with god knows what at the wheel. Though it does not seem to be within our relentless blueprint ever to completely die away.

Oil. Black gold.

And there are some that might remember another black gold upon these shores at one time though not a time out of mind. A black gold that would weep and fall in love with one another and sing a music soft in the twilight. It seems the podiums have all been torn away but the auction has never really ended. The one has replaced the other, as the boy flagbearer will bend to hold up the tattered burden of his dead confederate and what a burden it is, though the boy, the quick and the dead, will never see the true reason for his being on that battlefield, he sees the colors and the chrome and it pours a love into his heart and for that alone he is beautiful and young forever. The one has replaced the other and the auction finds itself at the gas station these days with the numbers fluctuating overnight under the quiet and cover of dark. Funny how the rise and fall of pennies can affect the way we feel about a given day. But the pump fits so nice into the orifice of the Ford or whatever. Sex has always sold but not sex alone. The pump itself being shaped not only like our male member but also like our hand-held revolver and where would we ever be without that duo?

I can't see the oil fields through the window anymore, only the land. And here I am convinced that if I could ever believe in America it would be only her wild blood that I'd believe in, not her banner never her banner no matter how broad the stripes, how bright the stars; her bad art on a tablecloth to which we've attached everything that we are, everything that we might someday be. And how could those stars ever be expected to endure stitched on in their one dimension with never a chance to burn as does their myriad namesake all over the night sky. But maybe they will have their moment to burn because isn't it in the nature of the star itself to burn out and fall down when its time has come? Fall in that dark theater and in this one? Fall without protest because of the knowing in its middle that there is and will be an order to things.

———

It is September outside, I believe, though I'm not sure. And this engine has brought me to the coastline. Two seabirds circling one another there above the water with nothing but the wind and the motive of wind to choreograph. The beauty aside, there seems to be some pressing trouble upon the hearts of these birds and though the trouble is for those hearts alone, I think I feel it here in my own body because I too have known how it is to be that way.

A man is running up and down the beach with a small girl, both of them holding in their hands a bundle of string tethered to the kites above. One yellow, one deep red.

A good distance down the coast is an old lighthouse wasting away with all or most of its windows gone. The lamp is dead. Not long before dark it had begun to rain and now it is falling hard. I would love to stop this train and jump out into the sand and with my own hands and a few simple tools somehow bring a life once more into the lighthouse. So that there might be some beacon for the lost to follow in all the dark. But I haven't got it in me. I can not stop this engine no more than I can stop the rain against the windows. But I know soon there will come a softer rain to follow after the downpour, with only a brief intermission between. So that the world might have a blue moment of rest. A small time to be alone and broken hearted.

Untitled

It made him sad to think that someday he'd die. September has a way of letting people know how it will feel when they are old when they are young. They don't see that this is so, but it is. They watch the light dying early and the leaves steady dying; they watch these things go, sigh and hope to see it all again. It is the hinting that is lost on them; chances for readying. And so, in the end, they fear it when it comes. They kick to the last.

Luna

1

Luna's been walking for years

all the endless highway that never was and now
is America

Luna has no eyelids

she's been watching the world for all this time

wide open

and it's no surprise to see her finally losing
touch

there's a crazy in the way she moves

like an animal in a summer dress on the side of
the road

sometimes she's on the yellow lines

Luna doesn't seem to notice the automobiles at
all anymore

2

Luna has a special something

a glass jar filled with ears

all different kinds

all different sizes

preserved forever in a golden liquid, a mixture

floating and sinking like strange seahorses

an ugly man gave her the jar

a gift in the back of a gas station nowhere in Alabama

and he says to Luna: —I got this here from a circus man. Always thought it had to be the prettiest thing, all golden...and golden. But I been a fool, I let it know all of everything...and I plumb run out of secrets. I plumb dried up.

the ugly man hands the golden jar to Luna and she takes it

he has a broken face and he smells like dogs

and fuel

and other things

but Luna sees a beautiful someone

precious underneath the fabric

precious underneath the skin

—Close your eyes, she says.

he does

and she kisses the ugly man soft on both eyelids

—Keep them closed for a while, she says. —
Please Mr. Gas Station...let me know how it feels
to have them down.

the ugly man juggles some words: —It feels
like...like midnight. Like cotton. Like butterflies.
It feels like nothing at all. And it feels like God.

Luna smiles and a tear moves down her face

like a quiet parade to the chin

then like the lemming...off the end of the chin
down to nowhere

—That's what I thought, whispers Luna.

the air changes

a busted radio that hasn't worked for thirty years begins to sing on the floor of the gas station

Luna presses the golden jar against her breast and walks away

the ugly man calls to her from the door and his voice is like the hinges of the door: —Careful what you let you let it know, child! Don't you go dryin' up like old me. Highway don't give a damn if you a girl or a dirty magazine. Pages fall to pieces...same as fingers and toes.

she doesn't listen

Luna only feels the warm of the jar against her body

only hears the radio

the radio

3

Luna hasn't rested her legs since she left the gas station

the pennyshoes and summer dress have fallen away into the landscape

she doesn't need them anymore

she is skin now and nothing else

the golden jar of ears pressed against her body like a glass infant

strange breastfeeder

no clocks out here on the highway

no difference to her in the shift in the shift between the dark and the day

time wears a changed and different costume when there's no way to close your eyes

a thing roars past Luna in the night

Oldsmobile

the horn and the curses from the window are angry and loud but it all seems completely different to Luna

like a harpsichord

like a children's song

—I love those silly monsters, she says to the ears. —The way they sing and their big bright eyes.

she knows the golden jar will always listen when she whispers all the delicate secrets of her insides it will never laugh

never spit

she breathes and the tail lights disappear into the black

a thought comes to Luna: —I had half a million secrets...once upon a time ago.

she counts on her fingers

—Now I have only one.

her feet stop

the fear is in her

the secret is in her belly

moving

climbing like a tiny trapezeman up the naked ladder of her body

but she wants to save it

he's in her throat now

hold on forever to it

he's on her tongue now

the tiny trapezeman chalks his palms and grabs the bar and now he swings out into the gravity amazing in the soft shoes

stupendous in the perfect-fitting purple and yellow suit

the secret hovers above the highway and her voice sounds like a woman and not like a woman

Luna belongs to a chemistry that we haven't touched yet

a type of baby girl that has never been born yet

listen to her soft broadcast: —I have no idea how old I am.

The Way Down

She jumped off the bridge.

On the way down she thought about laughter.

How it lasts.

So many different kinds.

Two new lovers under the powerlines. Laughing and tearing and sweating as they go. Honeysuckle on the lips, honeysuckle under the bellyline. The wires above them. The promise.

Three men in a room. Laughing over dividends. Starched laughter. Bleached white laughter. Laughter like numbers. Faces like posters. Raving and sweating as they go.

The crowd watches the idiot cross the street. They laugh. Jeer. His head is swollen. His eyes like milkweed. His hair, infested. The look of his clothes. The breadth of his memory. No belt. No gold. No bread. No friend in all the world. His ape hands. His ape hold. His back wrenched over by the cold inertia of his ape road. His dumb song. His locked up glory. His sleeping opus.

His kind eyelids. His kind pace. His untouched heart. His springtime soul. The crowd would love to see him on his face. The crowd is ill at ease and empty and sweating as they watch him go.

Old friends laughing in the rain.

Somewhere between laughter and her body breaking against the concrete water she began to think about hell.

The pictures they show us.

The screaming stillness of the pictures.

Eight Subsequent Rooms

> This case of blindness, the physician says,
> resulted from ophthalmia. It was really caused
> by a dark, overcrowded room, by the indecent
> herding together of human beings....
> —Helen Keller

1

There is an open bottle of tequila. Can you see it?

A small yellow bird perched on the shoulder of a dreamer. It smells like yesterday in this place. This octagon room painted blue: the color of sex and odd geometry.

On the wall is pinned a poster of a pregnant woman, nude except for boots to work the pedals of her bicycle, Persian language all along the border.

2

A small window.

Emily. Purple and gold polka-dot stockings. Eight and a half years old.

Flypaper glued to the blades of an obsolete ceiling fan. There is a man in the corner with a sketchpad. They call him the Cartoonist. They say the way that he smells means more than his name: like girls and sawdust.

3

Nothing but a mustard-colored sofa. And something else that you can't see. The ghost of a man. A filmmaker. Every now and again there is the silk screen of his body showing pale against the wallpaper.

The wallpaper has changed in its aspect. At one time it had been a very lovely color, decorated with the same little little girl painted in a thousand different postures. A thousand different hats.

But now there is what appears to be crayon all over everything. The same statement again and again. Small or not small or horizontal or backward or upside down. It reminds us of some strange and flexible dunce in front of a blackboard. A fevered and demented graffiti all over the ceiling and the walls.

We're going to make you a movie star.
We're going to make you a movie star.

4

Come into the barn. Ten thousand hoses have acquired the sickness and lived and died and given birth and been born in this barn forever. But all the horses have gone away. And we remember them now in the same detached fashion that we remember the pterodactyl...the zeppelin.

But the smell of the hoses is still here. Held over from a lost moment of agriculture. That pleasant ferment of vegetable compound and animal sex.

And we become curious now. Curious to know what new thing will be here to breath in the smell of the people when the smell of the people is all over everything long after the extinction has taken us away.

5

One proletariat housewoman in her hurry has placed five empty colored glass bottles against the windowpane. She has never considered herself to be any sort of luminary.

But here comes the sun.

And all the light from the outside shines through the window and in turn through the bottles and their subsequent colors are cast to the far and opposite corners of the floor. Like actors. Like refugees.

6

At one time this warehouse had been filled with boxes and boxes of rotary telephones.

But not anymore.

The warehouse has recently changed hands and there is a new owner now. A small and quiet landlord who never takes off his extravagant hat so that there are few people who have ever truly seen his face and there is no one that knows what his name is.

The main storage room is empty now except for one thing in the center of the floor and that thing is covered by an enormous white sheet and there is no way of guessing what is under the sheet. Only the landlord knows. He has been anticipating the correct time for the great unveiling of his conception and when he does the people will come from everywhere to see what it is that this man has made.

Men have experimented. Yes they have. But they have never gone this far. The small landlord has found a way to contain within this one thing a terrible fusion. Some despicable new science which has negotiated a brave marriage between religion and simple machinery and organic life and several other components that are without form and without title.

And soon the sheet will be lifted. And of course the people will cheer. They will hold up their children to see and in turn the children will cheer in their own ignorant soprano and there will be a fine harmony produced within those lofty acoustics of the warehouse.

And the thing that the landlord has made will be very popular. Yes, it will be a unanimous favorite. And the thing will be made again. And then it will be made again. And there will be no end to the systematic and corrupted reproduction. No end ever to that rotten and factoryesque impersonation of original love-making.

Why has there always been this sick curiosity? Was it with us in the cave? Was it here before we came? Did it hide itself in that fertile darkness of the beginning...waiting in quiet advertisement for some virgin species foolish enough to let it inside?

7

Someone has left the television on.

A department store clock against the wall says 4:10 but it has always said 4:10.

An imitation gold birdcage is hanging suspended from the ceiling but there is no bird inside and now the cage swings from one side to the other like a swollen runaway neglected three days in the tree or like some unorthodox pendulum that has been hung in this place to keep something other than time...something very different than time.

8

First we smell the soap and then we notice a young mother bathing her infant in the kitchen sink.

Her First Typewriter Dream

This dream of hers begins with the lowering of her body in order to hold the typewriter in both hands to lift it up above her head. It weighs nothing.

And so comes the familiar clicking of letters and digits and punctuation but it is not her fingers doing the typing. It is nothing doing the typing.

The instrument balanced above the body of her, held up like an offering to some god or other but there is no god in this dream. There is a painted sky and a painted sky is all.

Now the sounds and the desperate aspect of the typing dies away, as if they were never, and for the first time the machine takes on weight. More weight than our dreamer has known in her waking world. And so she lets the typewriter fall back down to the floor from where she had first taken it up. A sheet of paper there now in the mouth of the thing where no paper had been before.

Should she read it? Should she believe in the paper?

These Days

Sunday

listen

somewhere a record is skipping

a voice from the speaker has been repeating the same thing for a number of days

sounds like something heard in the belly of a crazy house

some piece of a lovesong turned frantic

as if the machine and the needle itself had some desperate message for mankind

there's a girl on the floor

her apricot blouse is showing more than she'd like to show

why hasn't she adjusted the needle or shut down the record player and put an end to the over and over and over?

Goodbye, Amelia.

the girl is dead

Thursday

a sunrise has done something to the lake

given it an aspect that reminds us of some time
after the end of the world

the murderer is out there in a canoe on the
middle of it

he is a very tall and thin man

he thinks of himself as the Longman

his hands are folded on his lap and his legs are
crossed

like some delinquent version of a monk or a holy
man

he is whistling

such an empty whistle in this wayplace

his mother had sung this same tune in the
mornings when he was a boy but there had been
words on the tune then

the song had been part of the chemistry of the
kitchen

an element as necessary as the things frying on
the stove

as intricate as the flypaper and the smell of the
milk

but the murderer has taken his mother's song
and made it his own

it is a thin whistle now

and it has no words these days

and all the milk has gone bad

look

a blackbird has taken flight in the direction of
the Longman and the canoe

a more refined and gentle aircraft than Amelia
and her people could have ever made

there's something in its beak

the blackbird lands on the canoe and drops the
something at the murderer's feet

a tiny figurine

the murderer is curious enough to lift it from the
bottom of the canoe with his fingers and his
fingers are long

it takes him a period of time to recognize what it is

the figurine is a miniature replica of himself

no bigger than a new embryo

incredible detail: the lines on the forehead—the birthmark

the blackbird has been watching the murderer

see the little spasm of its head?

more like an idiot savant than like any winged creature that we know

now the blackbird watches the Longman stand in the canoe and stretch his hands in the direction that he supposes heaven to be

he's holding up the toy replica of himself

he is in want of answer though his question is not intended for heaven

if the question is for anyone it is for he himself or for the person that used to be him

he's only asking and he doesn't expect an answer:

—Who made this?!

the murderer's cry is like a virus on the beauty
of the lake

some new polio against the quiet of the sunrise

and the blackbird does has an answer for the
murderer

it speaks perfect English from the edge of the
canoe:

—No one made it.

Almost Overnight

And we should believe that there are things to come in this world which are so very different from our ten thousand fancied assumptions of a Jetsonian future.

Through circumstance many of the instruments that we've cast away so quick in favor of all things plugged into the wall will again return to our everyday almost overnight. Pencils or candles or wooden shoes or otherwise. And this retrospective will not come in the name of fashion. No trend. It will be bare need.

And soon after, we will begin to name our children Penicillin, girl and boy alike, in hopes that by the sheer ritual of calling its name out daily this vanished medicine may someday come again to save us. Or perhaps a stronger medicine. Or if there is any mercy left in the world, any medicine at all.

And fresh water will be the new currency. And this tender will be worldwide. And there will be no stock market other than skinny livestock or perhaps whatever stock we might still hold in the cheap belief that America would last forever.

Simone Felice

The Washington

someone is selling something

picture the salesman

no textiles on him

this one is a naked manchild

ten years old and seven feet tall

back and forth and back and forth and back and
forth in a rockingchair at the crossroads

not the type of crossroads that we remember
from the western movie...another type

listen to the wind

sounds like an opera

sounds like a microwave

you followed that sound from somewhere
nowhere and it brought you here

the hands of the salesman are two very different sizes

in the small hand is an hourglass

the sand in the top is gone

filled up the bottom half

what could that mean?

there is a briefcase in the large hand

the salesman whistles: b flat

you see the actual note hover metal and real in front of his lips and then change into a tiny helicopter and go away

the briefcase opens on its own

there's a miniature city inside

the salesman smiles: —Perhaps I have something of interest? Something you might like to purchase? Welcome, beautiful one. Welcome at last to the sweet tomorrow.

you look down into this petite metropolis

pedestrians and motorcars

you see a pregnant woman on one of the boulevards

she's holding an umbrella and she looks familiar

it's your mother

you call down to her: What is this place?!

she looks up...screams and puts her fingers in her ears...drops the umbrella and runs into the miniature subway

scared to death of you

the god

the monster

the city disappears

and now there's something else in the briefcase

a marble

the same color as your mother's eye

how could this be?

you lost that marble in the drainpipe when you were nine

the salesman smiles one more time: — Perhaps I have something of interest? Something you might like to purchase?

remember how you used to talk to the marble sometimes when your mother would go away?

and it used to look you directly in the eye

you need to have it again, boy

you need it bad

reach into your pocket and produce a dollar bill

hand it to the salesman in exchange for the marble

but he doesn't seem to understand

—What version of currency is that? he asks

he doesn't recognize the washington

The Ballerina and the Wheelchair Man

The ballerina is under the impression that her crippled admirer loves her honestly for everything that she is. Loves her for what she does under the lights and for what he will never do in that wheelchair of his.

This man who brings flowers to the backstage.

And a time will come when he will not be afraid to invite her out on one of her off nights.

She will push him along to a small gallery that is a favorite of hers and there she will notice a changed aspect in the faces and postures of the figures in the sculpture room. She will have never noticed these aspects before and she will mention this curiosity to the cripple out loud.

Then she will push him along to the seaport and from the wooden pier they will look out onto the water where sailboats lie resting in the wet vibration of the harbor lamps like the ghosts of such boats and then she will take his hand in hers.

Goodbye, Amelia.

And after all this, in the same night, he will kill her. Kill her for her pretty shoes, intent to wear them on his own hands. And with these demented mittens now he will play the star. And he will shine on.

On the Sickman's Machine

7:47 AM— Sickman, won't you pull the drapes. They are red like your bloodbeat is red and the two will fall only to rise again, each in its own quiet way.

7:52 AM— Out past the drapes is the breaking spring. You are so far from her and this blood of yours is further still but she is not without her own reds. She comes as an eye in the dark and with it she knows the winter in you.

1:33 PM— Sickman, won't you hold on. Circumstance is your deadbride today and all the turning of the sky won't bring her back. There will be medicine in the morning, Sickman.

4:51 PM— Will you overlook the moth on the sill? Don't. You should go with him when he leaves. He has come to hide his loveliness under his skeleton but you will see it. Study the thing that he is and change into it or you will atrophy on past to where there is no coming home.

The Walker

1. *Give us the eyes so that we might one day see.*

I see a man in a birdcage.

I see a long equation but I have no idea what it is or how to begin.

I see the ghost of everything soviet, living without living, in between the spaces of the world around.

I see this pageant played over and over with only the costumes being updated, only the props and the backdrop changing as time goes on.

I see a woman with her throat cut, dead these ten days with ten fingers of her own.

I see Los Angeles wrapped up in a blanket of heartache and it seems that she is wasting away although sometimes the wasting away can feel warm and so good and I think I love her though I've never known her.

I see a bird wearing a gas mask over its head.

I see all the president's men.

I see whatever god is dying without proper witness in a bad bad baptism of oil and gasoline.

I see a world still reeling.

I see a world never not reeling.

2. *Give us the ears and the small hammers so that we might one day hear.*

I hear them coming.

I hear the lost and lonely cries of a monkey in space—monkey in space.

I hear the open highway calling out for me to live in transit from place to place but I don't believe I've been made with a heart for drifting.

I hear a low voice over the oval office telephone line and can anyone guess who's on the other end?

I hear the aeroplanes.

I hear seven billion children all engaged in the same game of Chutes and Ladders.

I hear an owl crying out against the night.

I hear the discharge of a rifle.

I hear no owl.

3. *Give us the lungs and the double barrel of the nose so that we might one day breathe in.*

I've breathed in the common fumes of a superpower, the pollen in the orchard.

I've breathed in the yellow dust, come to us in patterns of longing, patterns of difficult love, half alive and rising up from off the wreckage of the day.

I've breathed in the draft riot and by doing so became, myself, the draft riot.

I've breathed in all these wild things that grow.

I've breathed in and out inside a belly and so sometimes I feel lost in this place without my gills.

I've breathed in the perfect asbestos from the bottom of her back and I've come now to carry it with me wherever I go.

I've breathed in the smell of kings and queens and I never will again.

I've breathed in eleven years of memorabilia and through it came a lost friend...isn't that always the way?

4. *Give us the surface of the tongue so that we might one day savor.*

I taste the Vietnam.

I taste the rosemary.

I taste the hold, as quiet as breathing, unbroken and reaching out to all the bitter edges of the commonwealth.

I taste the coriander.

I taste the labia of War.

5. *Give us the heart and this barrier of skin so that we might one day feel.*

I feel the lips of consequence moving at will down my belly line.

I feel a shadow in the government, its quiet eclipse in all things—like a random bird, like a wind in the door.

I feel like a farm boy lost in Paris, my first time feeling ceiling fans.

I feel drunk.

I feel a vacancy in the constitution, she is tired... finding it hard to hold on through all the yellowing and yellowing away.

I feel the sun shining all through these dark ages.

I feel poised to inherit the degeneracy of my race and it hurts me more than I can say.

I feel the Fahrenheit bearing down.

6. *Give us the knowing.*

I know the footfalls of the walker have been ever gaining. Sure as a million year rain, beating a violent chronicle into the carbon of the highwayside. He has lost his way, this child of the sun. Orphaned up whatever grace was given to him, left it in the desert; himself an orphan of the howling space above his head. There will be no rest for the walker. He made fire in another world, a gone hour, and it is this same burning that calls him on. Back toward the birth of the empty where the end has been eating itself alive. On back until blood and gold are one.

Simone Felice

Pieces of the Carpenter

It wasn't loving. Loving was frightening.
Maybe it did not last. Maybe he would lose it.
— Ernest Hemingway
Summer People

We smell the animals and we see the figure of the Shepherd positioned there at the edge of the bluff like a dark and postured paper doll cut out against the sky and the night. The man and the plateau where he walks in his trade and his everyday have become one thing. Time has made the two conglomerate, an understood and quiet matrimony. One of them wears the dirt and the long grass. One of them wears the rags.

And down and down are all the lights of the city, no more than a cheap and adjustable manmade constellation when it's all said and done. But the Shepherd has come away from the city. Nothing at all anymore for him down in their dirty grid. He is here now in these empty upper parts, here with the sheep and their young ones, never taking the milk or the wool or anything else from them, keeping them only because he loves to watch them sleep and move and that is all.

———

The Carpenter is sleeping now. Somewhere down in the population he is alone and molded fetalesque in his blanket; a breathing specimen on the floor with the sawdust and the nails and the other simple things.

This night the Carpenter dreamt and in that dream he was again the boy he had been. Everything in the dream environment was accented in a washed-out red haze and the boy sat mounted upon the banana seat of a bicycle sweating and pedaling slow through traffic. The cars seemed all to part at his coming. No horns and no curses from the motorists. In fact no sounds at all but for a low and awkward piano music making its way into the frame from some unseen quarter of the dreamscape. The piano itself being completely out of tune.

The boy alternating his head to the side looking intermittently left and right in order to navigate because his mother is sitting like a rag doll on the handlebars. Delirious and bleeding from her wrists. This outlandish, today She-Christ being delivered to the city hospital by no other than her little son on his thin two-wheeled ambulance that should never be an ambulance and why does she not want to live anymore?

———

Close to the Carpenter's apartment and meanwhile, on a makeshift bed, there is blood between someone's legs and brand new life. Picture the fundamental one room where she lives and what more living is there than to be holding in the light bulb light the very same babe that had only some minutes ago been on the inside of you. Pressed against her heart and not wailing at all, this one, but sleeping sound. The sort of deserved sleep that we witness in the face of a fisherman finally returned to a real bed after a month or more out on the open sea and at the mercy of the tides of this world. The same tides that we are believed to understand and predict but in truth will never understand. Never those tides and certainly never the ones within us that have always moved us to do what we do.

—How does it feel, Aubergine? My Aubergine.

—I can't feel anything.

—It is a boy I think. It is a beautiful boy I think.

—It is a boy, isn't it?

—Yes.

—Did I cry much, Beekeeper?

—Wouldn't you know if you cried? If anyone knew wouldn't you be the one to know if yourself cried out in the middle of all this, my Aubergine?

—No. It didn't seem like I was here. I wouldn't have known if I had lived or died.

Aubergine had kissed boys before and once she had kissed a man but his mouth had tasted wrong like old coffee and another thing that she didn't know the name of and she never kissed that man again or any other man. Twice she had felt the moisture in that soft place between her upper legs and once her hand had found its way there like someone else's hand and had danced it's wet ballet of fingers and thumbs all over the threshold of that tissue while the ice in the water on the windowsill melted and with all the strange and good perfumes of summer making their way in and out of that same window.

Aubergine remembers no real penetration from even her and if not from her then from no one. So how did this boy wrapped in a tapestry against her heart come to begin his incubation?

There are several days in her recent life that are completely gone from her. As a young girl Aubergine had adopted the habit of always keeping a wall calendar. She would brand or mark every space within the square of that numbered day with a sort of personal code. The symbols would differ and change depending on the atmosphere of the day itself. Rain or sun or someone screaming down the street. Cold or hot or dry or perhaps there was some new fear or love in the air or in the sky. Any shift at all. So that there would always be a sort of beautiful and illiterate hieroglyphic pattern written in pencil all over the calendar and Aubergine had never missed a day in her life. Forever chronicling the various basic heart and frown and smile symbols and the rudimentary drawings of bird and animal shapes and the spirals and octagons and ovals and other simple geometrics that only she knew the meaning of.

If one could have watched her in the

evenings, standing almost hypnotized with her pencil scribbling and scribbling again, one might think this were some hectic and gentle religion that man has forgotten or that man never knew or that man remembers and pretends not to remember.

But one morning Aubergine woke and opened her eyes and she was standing erect in her one room. She was nude except for a pair of extraordinary shoes that she had never seen before and the first thing she did was to approach and examine her wall calendar. The most recent entry was on a day that she knew was not yesterday because she could feel this in her belly and she could feel something else in her belly and she ran out into the street to ask what day it was and she had never been so afraid.

———

We deserve a description of the small city where everyone lives. Only the Shepherd is not here but we know where he is. Some of the building facades are painted in solid bright colors and some are not. Paint or no paint, the stuff that the apartments and storefronts are made of is the same thing: a basic stucco spread over an endoskeleton of wood or metal or both.

All of these streets and avenues and their back alleys have come to lie in a kind of drunken arrangement, no obvious or logical civic planning, they build and they build again. A synagogue and a pawnshop and a pharmacy and a tabernacle and a whorehouse and a courthouse and all the other things that people need.

And there is art. One lone statue of a young man from one of the wars in front of the courthouse. He is eight feet tall and cast in a sort of running posture with his helmet and his rifle and his eyes on fire. He is not afraid. He is not afraid. He was bronze once but now he is green. A sad and diluted green that reminds us of the uniforms they use. It seems as though the rain and the chemistries of weather have made a fine irony here.

And all the names and names below him chiseled into the base stone, some industrial version of calligraphy. Easy. Easy and ugly. These are boys who used to swim and dream and never will again. They are names and nothing else now. Several meaningless syllables ignored by the passerby. This is the art that the city has made. No monument to love or sunlight or anything else that makes us live.

———

—Come down off that scaffold!

The Blue Lady calls up to the Carpenter. He climbs down. The Blue Lady is smiling. She loves how he talks when he talks to her, like a poor and gifted boy, timid and happy at the same time. She loves the way his hand shakes when she gives him his wages.

—Thank you, he says and takes the envelope.

He's looking mostly at his boots and at the tiles and sometimes at her.

—Thank you, lady, he says again.

—Go home now and be here in the morning.

She walks back the way she came, through the double doors and into the garden. The Carpenter is wet in the armpits as he watches the Blue Lady go. He loves her because he knows that she is so very different a thing than he is. He examines her big hat and wonders what it is made of. The Carpenter is exhausted, holding the envelope in both hands like an heirloom, like a newborn. Money is nothing to the Blue Lady. She's never thought about what it is. It has always been here and for her it will always be here like some vague and paper oxygen.

———

Walking home and now almost home he sees a girl with a baby in her arms up on one of the fire escapes. He's seen her before but they've never talked. Once she'd smiled at him and he returned the smiled but the Carpenter's smile is no smile at all. She looks different today. He had never noticed the infant child before and he wonders if it is new and if it is hers. She has an assortment of flowers tied up in her hair in such a wild and strange way as to make us think that this were the first time that a woman had ever tried such a thing, with no learned or practiced technique to this lovely multicolored prototype. It seems almost as if the stems and petals had come directly from out of the pores of her head, same as the hair itself, and were no work of vanity or fashion but simply the way things are and had always been.

———

Angel is an awkward word to use in this place in these days but there is a poverty in this language we've made and angel is all that there is. He is somewhere close to fourteen years old. He is tall for his age and skinny and there has always been a light in his eyes. The nature of the hair on his head is like to no other hair that people have seen. It moves when his head is still. It moves when there is no wind on the air. It moves when the child sleeps, like some life form stolen from the ocean floor and unable to abandon its culture here. No love for gravity. No love for vertebrae. We should remember the simple things on the dark bottoms. They have lived with a freedom that we have never known and will never know. They have been here since the world was made and we have not.

The child has a name and that name is Michael and Michael is in his room now at the end of a thin bed watching out the open window. A few feet from his window is a brick wall and another window with only the air between smelling of vehicles and people like the afflicted cast-off twin of air and somewhere above that chasm is the sky. The birds come in through Michael's window. The birds have always come in through Michael's window. They rest on his lean shoulders and on the top of his head and on his kneecaps as he sits. No less than twenty of them at a time. And not only the usual gray birds of the city, though they too are surely welcome, but different ones that have come out of the wilderness and colored ones that have come a long way.

—The Fat Man is good and beautiful.

Michael is talking to himself now and to the many birds.

—He is not my father from his own blood but he loves me and I love him. We have been with each other from the time when I was little but he was never little. That was what he said. He used to talk. He taught me words and the way to talk but then something happened to the Fat Man. I brought the doctor here. The doctor smelled clean but not good. He opened his black bag and metal things were inside and he took them out and looked into the Fat Man's eyes and into his mouth and then the doctor listened to his heart. He said that a bad thing had happened to the Fat Man and that he would stay there in his soft favorite chair for a long time until he died and then I would have to carry him out or else he would begin to smell. He said that the Fat Man would never talk again or understand words. The doctor said vegetable and then he went home.

The birds stirred in the room and some changed places and others moved closer to Michael as if they wished to comfort him or perhaps to better hear his story. The birds have never seen the Fat Man. He lives in the other room in his chair with his eyes always open looking into the purple glow of the broken television in front of him.

—I tried to talk to him and I tried kissing

his face and his hands and then I cried into my own hands. A long time after he turned quiet I was walking past him and out of the house but then I turned around and I looked at his face. Something was different. One of his eyes was wet and the wet was moving down. I came to him and I sat at his feet and I couldn't feel my body. It was so long since he showed me any living. Then a question came into my heart from nowhere and I asked it to the Fat Man: Why do you weep, Fat Man? I weep for the sins of the world. That was what the Fat Man said. And so it seems that this is all that he knows anymore, or maybe it's the only thing he'll say. It hurts not to go outside together anymore or sing or talk but I love him the same. And now every time I walk past him and the chair and the purple TV on my way outside or coming inside I ask the question, our question. And this is the only time he seems alive. His eyes change into happy eyes. Why do you weep, Fat Man? I weep for the sins of the world. And so it has turned into something like a nice game or like a good thing that always happens anyway even if the world is bad. Like the sun coming up. Or like babies. Or like the way I feel when it rains in the city in the summer after not raining for days and days and days.

———

The hinge on the door to the Carpenter's apartment has been broken in two for so long. The wind and what rides the wind comes out and comes freely in. You'd think he'd have fixed it by now. Why does it become so hard to do for ourselves what we do everyday under the watch and employment of others? Have they bled our time away? And if they have, what are we after all the bleeding is done?

———

—He drinks it. It comes from me. Out of my nipple. I am full with it. I am so empty.

———

The Blue Lady could hire a dozen gardeners. Import them from other parts of the world. Specialists in seed and leaf and flower. But she doesn't do that. The garden is hers to care for. Something about being on her knees with the dirt and the roots. Maybe it lets her feel simple. Like a peasant feels. Luckily she knows that she can always get off her knees if she begins to feel too ordinary and wash all of it off and away in the bath.

———

It must hurt not to tell what it is that you dream but this is the sad condition in which we find our Fat Man. He sees some colors and depth and small movement but it doesn't seem to mean a thing. He might not tell what it is that he dreams but this doesn't mean that we can't know.

Windmill. Windmill but no wind. Road sign. Why would there ever be a road sign in such an

*empty place where there is no road whatsoever?
See the girl sitting with her back against the
bottom of the windmill. All her flesh is laid bare to
us. All the new fuchsia. Everything smells like a
train station. Everything smells like an old
woman. Now there is a rifle in the girl's hands.
She turns her head toward the audience but her
face is not a face.*

The Fat Man wakes in his element. The
warm purple of his broken TV seems such a
peaceful thing after being where we just were.
Who is the girl? She's been in every one of his
dreams for so long now and she will not leave.
But it is only pieces of her in the dreams. Pieces
of her and pieces of what's happened to her.

––––––

It happens that at this moment the Blue
Lady is on her knees in her garden with a belly
full of amphetamines. What she's planted this
year has come up and they are all in their rows
but there is no life in them. After an hour or so
spent in vain manipulation of soil she hears
through the courtyard the sounds of the
Carpenter. He is up on the scaffold with a fine
piece of hickory using his hand plane to work
the piece though there are outlets enough on the
premises for a thousand power tools. The Blue
Lady follows the faint sound and soon she is
standing under the Carpenter.

—Come down, monkey!

The soft noise of metal against wood stops
in mid-plane and so does the Carpenter's heart.
He had been called this before and more then

forty years ago but not by her. Not this daughter of gross industry. Inheritor of more than just her father's gold. For days he has been giving everything he is into the wood around those upper windows; his life unto the moldings. And this is more than the Carpenter can bear. He comes down. Blue Lady moves away from the ladder quicker than you'd think she could, sidestepping like a drunken athlete. Looking into his eyes as he passes her she sees for the first time the hunger in his face. The boy inside.

She watches him go down the driveway. Striding like some exiled statesman leaving forever the corrupt and ungrateful parliament to which he's leased and so wasted the better portion of his life.

It is hard for her to see him now with the water in her eyes and just before he passes the gates she sees or thinks she sees something fall from his waist and it is not until the next morning that her doorman finds the tool belt lying in the dirt like a broken pilgrim, yellow with the sickness and left for dead.

———

—Why this life, Beekeeper?

—This garden grows the way it will, Aubergine. We are not the gardener. We would never fit into those rubber boots.

—Stay with us a while.

—The hive calls, love.

—Don't go away. Not yet.

But the Beekeeper is already gone with all the guilt of his warped brand of infidelity rising up in his chest on his way down the fire escape.

———

The Carpenter makes his way on foot out of the city proper. Past factories. Past farms with their silos high and proud like the towers of some lost city where dead corn feed was no less a god than the sun itself. The livestock through the fences watching his progress until he is lost and gone from view out of whatever limits lay upon the bovine vision. And one by one these animals return to their grazing with the sorrow growing urgent and swollen on their hearts because that man and the countless gone before him, all long now down the road, have passed and passed without making himself known as the One, fabled among the farmyard, who had come to save them. Come upright and mighty to swing open the gates and free them. Though somewhere inside they know without question that they would every one of them return the morning after even before the sun, trotting back through those same gates, starving and cotton-mouthed and half crazy for fear of a night just spent outside but more afraid of a life without a keeper to direct them and pacify.

Moving on through sunshine and though shade, the Carpenter. All the air of late summer on and around his face. When was the last time he smelled the world? The free and living world?

In time the land begins to rise and with increasing drama so that if he were to look back he would see the city, petite and alien, down in the low country. But he does not look back and he does not turn back or quit the road although now it is hardly a road. The trees are small up here but they are strong, hugging the dirt lane like a long sideline of mute onlookers to this slow and lonely marathon. Soon he is following the narrow footpaths through the brush made by the wild things in those woods. Birds watch him come and watch him go, turning their special necks in a matter of fact way as if they'd been already told of his passing in a dream.

————

—Why do you weep, Fat Man?

A breeze comes in through the window and touches them both, moving a mustard curtain aside, an instant later replacing it.

—I weep for the sins of the world.

————

It is such a small garden she's made up here on her fire escape, if in fact it can be called a garden. A tomato plant. Some tiny flowers and three sunflowers. Half a dozen ferns in a bucket. A sort of ivy on the railing. Simple, but all of it alive with a kind of living that has been extinct in this city since time out of mind. This afternoon the blood sun has fallen behind a family of clouds, low in the almost evening sky. It will show itself again.

She is sitting in a found wicker chair, her baby son in her arms. The chair is stained an off off white from all the rain and whatever we've put into the rain but it is a comfortable chair.

Aubergine is bending her lips to his ear, sharing with him things that she always believed were secret and now important for her to pass on. She tells him of an animal called the seahorse and how hard it is for the mother seahorse to bring her babies into the world. She tells him of how tired the mother is following the birth and of all the sleep she needs afterward and how it has always been the way of these animals for the father to attach the babies onto his hooked tail and with his soft train in tow the father will go about hunting for the small foods underwater that keep the family alive and then she tells the boy that he himself has no father in this world.

—There is no way for you not to become part of their thing now that you're here on the outside.

Her fingers tighten themselves close together and the small muscles over the bones of her face move and changed a little.

—But I will put the love into you. I will put it in you even if it cripples me. Even if it makes me old before I am.

————

The hives of his devising on the rooftop of his building have all been arranged in loose rows over time; a smaller, sweeter skyline of his own. The Beekeeper is walking between them with an air of great purpose, stopping at this one or that in order to make any small adjustment or simply to look down at the given box with a fond scrutiny. The swarm about the body of the Beekeeper covering his head and torso in a frantic cloud of living copper and so rendering his face anonymous inside the log and files of mankind and perhaps this man would in truth have wished it so. The skin of his hands and face exposed. No need to parade around like a moon man or like a student of fencing or like some stupid merger of the two; he is hardly ever stung and if he is he welcomes the sting with a queer half-smile, the kind foster father of this small and gorgeous monarchy.

But how many nights gone by without rest? How many nights weeping into hands or pillowcase until the sad reservoir behind the face lay baron? And after all the evaporating the sadness being nonetheless until it seemed like chalk dust might come falling from the eyes. Not falling to appease the broken will of the Beekeeper but being sent directly by some unreckoned dispatcher, an assurance of tears, a dry surrogate offered to avoid any chance of insult to the very office of woe, that office holding full jurisdiction over a place like this.

The little queen inside the hive could never love him and this is tearing the Beekeeper apart. All this weeping because he loves the little queen with a love unbearable. A love ridiculous. His stomach hurts. He would give anything to know what drones she brings into her bed and at what hour. What odd lusts they satisfy in that humid place within the comb. It eats him up inside, all the not knowing. But could she feel the same for him in her wings and yellow velour? Could she be meanwhile longing for the Beekeeper? That bodiless voice that calls now and then from out of her low heaven. And would he know her if she came to him in another form? This form. If she were to pass him on the street, in a hallway, would he know her then? Or she him? With her new eyes, still learning how to work this body like something just out of a coma, out of a cage. Would she feel the tug and pull of those same things that tug and pull at our hearts and ours alone among the creatures of the earth? Could the queen ever relinquish her position for a life lonely with a man? This man? Could she ever let go of the pomp, the dead ceremony of the throne?

———

Bad laughter. Who is it in the shadows? Birds are flying above the windmill but they are flying backwards. See the outline of a dunce cap on the silhouetted head of the hiding man. He has done something. Folly. The usual girl is more animated then she's ever been. Dancing a frantic, mindless pirouette around and around the windmill. Bare naked again. Though not wholly naked. Shoes. Gold sequined knee-high footwear. Thin double high heels. Folly. A mean wind is tearing across the land. Through the dream. Tearing through the girl. But she is dancing. Folly. Dancing and the hiding man is hiding.

———

—Make it go away.

———

—There's a trouble in his head. I know it. Someone else's troubles. One that eats itself alive. His warm feels vacuumed away. I know warm. He showed it to me in the field. I was so small but I remember the yellow.

In the room the birds breathe as birds do. He's tired. He takes hold of the lamp and unplugs it from the wall but the lamp inside his person burns on and will not be put out, should a longer night come, should all the wrong of the earth surround him. The Fat Man has cared for him, raised him up, and now Michael is here to care for the Fat Man as if there could be any other way.

—Trouble.

———

The Carpenter is lost now but the Carpenter is free. He's had nothing to eat for more than a week in the wild and his eyes have gone wild at the edges. Once he thought he heard his mother calling his name out through the night and once he was sure he saw her running in frolic from tree to tree, hiding like a schoolgirl in the forest ahead. He chased her for hours in that empty place though in truth what he chased was nothing. Dead echoes. But to the Carpenter, in those hours, it was everything. What more truth could there ever be than to follow the strings of the heart? Hunger dreams or none.

Today is raining so hard and by now he has lost most of his clothes and one of his boots but he doesn't appear to give a goddamn. The frequency of trees has diminished and the ones that remain in these elevations are dwarfed and sad. By and by, the Carpenter comes into a clearing; a sort of upland meadow where the rare flowers of the place and season seem to hold a placid dominion over all. In his rough beard and sorry outfit he might have come to be mistaken as a dirty visitor wandered out of an older time, a fallen king or a madman. But there is no jury in this high lonely place. No witness to the Carpenter's passing. Or is there?

A sole being is out at the edge of the meadow where the cliffs begin and end, with his face and his hands pointed up toward the downpour in apparent defiance of weather and the origin from where all weathers come. Defiance or communion, who could tell? The Carpenter walks toward him and sees the view upon which this man has fixed himself in the driving rain. Beyond the bluffs and far down below is the city.

—They hung a man at the courthouse today, he cries out to the Carpenter without turning his head or lowering his arms.

—Hung him for running free and nude through the streets. For shouting nonsense out loud. Hung him for showing what was in his heart. The queer one. The one not meant for this world. The one she calls the Beekeeper.

—She who?

—You know who. She is on the courthouse lawn. Hysterical. Holding up the boy to see their dead friend punished as he is.

—What boy?

—There are rules, Carpenter. Rules.

Everyone is at the hanging. Who could miss a hanging? Why are you not there with them? What was it that you hoped to find? Have you come here whistling for liberty? Did you seek to tough it? Hold it? Liberty is nowhere.

———

It is full of secrets. It's been a best friend.

—You will be on the other side of the umbilical this time around...yes?

This broken dog is the one talking. It should be dead. It might be dead.

—The other side this time...

She is listening good, the girl, her knees pulled tight against her chest, squatting beside this dog she's never seen. The windmill turns round. What is it that's been written on the road sign all this time?

—I have lungs and you have lungs, explains the animal. There is little that separates us.

The girl breathes; the dog smells wrong.

—What is written on the road sign is written all through our blood. I love you...as he loved you, in his way. Don't presume he's gone for good.

The windmill turns round and the broken dog talks on, full of secrets.

———

Everyone has gone home, abandoned the body of the Beekeeper, streaker deviant felon, to turn alone on its sorry axis. Clockwise for the young. Counter for the pleas of the old. Back the other way for the wind.

The sun is gone. The windows of the courthouse are dark. The rain is done. Aubergine's sheets have been kicked down to the end of the bed. She's been asleep. Sleep without peace. The boy is nearly three feet tall, standing over his mother like a miniature physician in too big pajamas watching her exhale and twitch with his feet on the mattress. Today he saw the first hanging of his life through the green eyes he has in the light of day. This night he'll say his first word. His mother wakes at the sound of it.

—Home.

It sounds far away. Virgin distant trachea. He says it again. More inquiry than revelation. Is this not what we've all longed for? Laughter downstairs, shoes familiar by the door? Something to hold when everything else has turned to shadow and camouflage. Home. Aubergine sits up in bed, shakes away the dream she was in, and pulls the boy close to her. Pain does not sleep, it anticipates the morning. But there are other things that wake with the sun, lighter things, and it might be that they are not so far away.

Under the Magnolia Tree

Under the magnolia tree we forgot our names awhile and cursed our wounds until our wounds ran off crying into the night, leaving us free to sing out.

And so we sang for the fornicators.

Sang for the friendship we've shared.

Sang for the left behind.

For the battered saints in the field.

The slaves.

The sad.

The pulled apart.

We sang for the blood-colored sky out past the branches.

Under the magnolia tree we kissed and rolled and sang out loud for the scared boy inside the general.

Goodbye, Amelia.

Sang for the general inside the priest.

The priest inside the poet.

The poet in the thief.

The thief in the angel.

The angel in the bombardier.

The bombardier in the dancer.

The dancer in the amputee.

The amputee who hides aching inside every last one of us.

About the Author

Simone Felice was born in Palenville, New York, in 1976. He writes today in the related disciplines of fiction, poetry, and song. His work has appeared in journals and on sound recordings internationally.

Felice has traveled extensively, giving readings in theaters, bookstores, schools, and cafés in North America and Europe.

His first book of poetry, *The Picture Show*, was published in 2000 by Hunger Press. An album, *The Big Empty* (SuperStar Label), was released in 2002, featuring the work of his songwriting collective.

Felice remains in the Hudson River Valley, not far from where he was born.

About the Artist

Jordin Isip was born and raised in Queens, New York. Since receiving a BFA from Rhode Island School of Design he has resided in Brooklyn, New York. Jordin's mixed-media images have appeared in numerous periodicals including *Adbusters*, *The Atlantic Monthly*, *Bloomberg Personal Finance*, *The New York Times*, *Rolling Stone*, *Time Magazine*, and *Yahoo! Internet Life* as well as on book covers, posters, records and CDs. He is currently teaching at Tyler School of Art and Rhode Island School of Design.

Jordin Isip's work has received awards from and publication in annuals including American Illustration, The Art Directors Club, Communication Arts, Print Magazine, and The Society of Publication Designers. In addition, he has shown his work in solo and group exhibitions in Los Angeles, New York, Philadelphia, San Francisco, Ontario, and Rome.